CAESAR'S LEGIONS

THE ROMAN SOLDIER 753BC TO 117AD

CAESAR'S LEGIONS

THE ROMAN SOLDIER 753 BC TO 117 AD

TEXT BY

NICHOLAS V SEKUNDA   SIMON NORTHWOOD   MICHAEL SIMKINS

COLOUR PLATES BY

RICHARD HOOK   ANGUS McBRIDE   RON EMBLETON

OSPREY
HISTORY

First published in Great Britain in 2000 by Osprey Publishing,
Elms Court, Chapel Way, Botley, Oxford OX2 9LP, United Kingdom
Email: osprey@osprey-publishing.co.uk

Previously published as Men-At-Arms 283 *Early Roman Armies*,
Men-at-Arms 291 *Republican Roman Army 200-104BC* and
Men-at-Arms 46 *The Roman Army from Caesar to Trajan*

ISBN 1 84176 044 7

Editor: Nikolai Bogdanovic

Filmset in Singapore by Pica Ltd
Printed in China through World Print Ltd

00 01 02 03 04   10 9 8 7 6 5 4 3 2 1

FOR A CATALOGUE OF ALL TITLES PUBLISHED BY
OSPREY MILITARY, AUTOMOTIVE AND AVIATION PLEASE WRITE TO:

The Marketing Manager, Osprey Direct UK, PO Box 140, Wellingborough,
Northants NN8 4ZA, UK
Email: info@OspreyDirect.co.uk

The Marketing Manager, Osprey Direct USA, P.O. Box 130,
Sterling Heights, MI 48311-0130, USA
Email: info@OspreyDirectUSA.com

OR VISIT OSPREY'S WEBSITE AT:
http://www.osprey-publishing.co.uk

FRONT COVER Gemma Tiberiana copy after the cameo of the
Glorification of Germanicus, by Peter Paul Rubens (1577 – 1640).
(Courtesy Ashmolean Museum, University of Oxford)

CONTENTS

ROME'S EARLY HISTORY

Early Rome and the Romans were only one of a number of peoples and settlements in Iron Age Italy. From the earliest historical times Rome fell under the influence of her powerful Etruscan neighbours to the north, and, indeed, throughout most of the sixth century BC Rome was ruled by kings, the Tarquins, who came originally from the Etruscan city of Tarquinii. In 509 (according to later Roman tradition) the last of these Etruscan kings, Tarquinius Superbus, was expelled. Rome declared herself a Republic, and was governed by two annually elected magistrates known as 'consuls'. For a while, how-

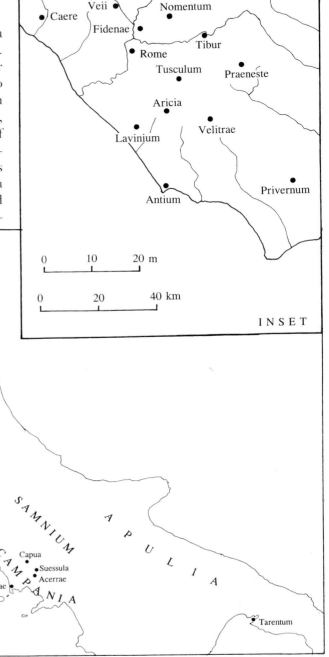

ever, Rome fell under the control of Lars Porsenna of Clusium. Porsenna was defeated at Aricia in *c.* 504 by an alliance between Rome, other Latin peoples and Aristodemus of Cumae. However, Rome was left in a weakened position and the Latins refused to accept Roman hegemony instead embarking on a war against her. This ended with a Roman victory at Lake Regillus (variously 499 or 496), but, although Rome was victorious, the settlement with the Latins, known as the Cassian treaty, seems to have been more of a compromise than a return to the previous situation of Roman dominance.

Latium at this time was increasingly threatened by a number of Apennine hill tribes. A common defensive alliance was agreed which aimed at presenting a united front against them. How the alliance worked in practice is difficult to tell given the scarcity and unreliability of our historical source material. All the Latin communities, including Rome, will have

provided troops, but who commanded them? One literary fragment from the first century BC Roman antiquarian Cincius implies an annual command rotating between the various members of the alliance. Much of the fifth century BC saw Rome at war alongside the Latins defending Latium against the Sabines, Volsci and Aequi who were eager to settle in more fertile territory. In this endeavour the alliance seems to have been largely successful and in the later part of the century former territorial losses were being recovered.

Not all Roman warfare was organized as part of the Latin alliance. The security of Rome's northern border was essentially her own responsibility, and this involved protection against the closest Etruscan city, Veii, which was situated twelve miles north-east of Rome on the opposite bank of the Tiber. Rome was at war with Veii in 483–474 (during which time there occurred a famous Roman defeat at the battle of

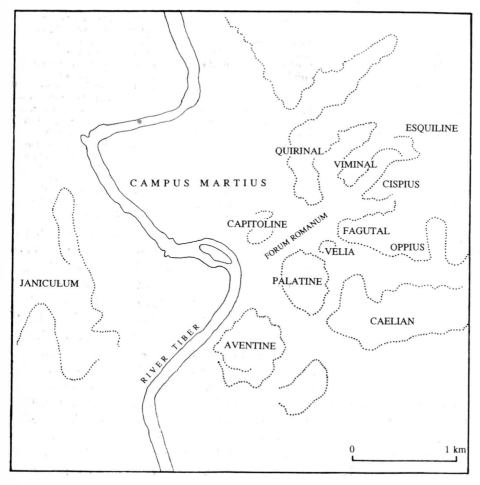

At Rome the River Tiber has cut a deep valley into the local tufa rock about a mile across. Some of the hills of Rome, the Capitoline, the Palatine and Aventine, lie in this valley separated from its sides, while others, the Caelian, Oppian, Esquiline, Viminal and Quirinal, are spurs connected to the valley sides. The Tiber flows in two loops, the northern one containing the marshy Campus Martius.

Cremera). Conflict began again intermittently in the 430s until the Veientine satellite colony of Fidenae was destroyed in 426. The most important conflict with Veii, however, began in 406 and lasted for ten years, at the end of which Veii was conquered by the Roman general Camillus. Veii was destroyed and her territory seized. This was a most significant development since it was the first time Rome had destroyed and occupied an enemy state of comparable size.

Rome's expansion was temporarily halted by the Gallic incursion of Brennus, during which the city of Rome was sacked following a crushing defeat at the Allia (traditional date 390 BC). Rome's long term position seems not to have been unduly damaged, however. Indeed an extended period of aggression, which had begun with the war against Veii, continued with the recapture of the Pomptine district of Latium from the Volsci and the annexation of the nearby Latin community of Tusculum in 381.

Rome's next major wars were undertaken against the Latin towns of Tibur and Praeneste. These had never been part of the Latin League allied to Rome, but they now posed a threat to Roman dominance in Latium, perhaps as champions of the Latins against Rome. Both towns were finally defeated in 354. Shortly afterwards concurrent wars in Etruria reached a successful conclusion: forty year truces were granted to Caere in 353 and to Tarquinii and Falerii in 351.

Rome now had no serious challenger in Latium and possessed a secure northern border with Etruria. Her next entanglements were to draw her into operations in new theatres. In 343 the peoples of Campania appealed to Rome for help against the Samnites, a powerful group of tribes who inhabited the central southern highlands of Italy. Rome intervened on behalf of the Campanians and the conflict was concluded in 341.

That same year the Latins finally rebelled against Rome and united themselves with the Volsci. This was a serious rebellion but it was suppressed by 338, in which year the Romans fundamentally reformed their relationship with the Latins and their other allies. Many communities lost their independence and became *municipia* with Roman citizenship; others negotiated new treaties with Rome and still others received a new status (the *civitas sine suffragio* or 'citizenship without the vote') which imposed all

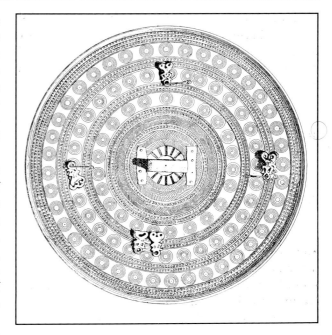

Ornamental shield from Esquiline Tomb 94. This shield was probably manufactured in Etruria, possibly in Tarquinia which was a major manufacturing centre. Like other Etruscan 'Parade-Shields' of this period, the Esquiline shield was of extremely thin sheet bronze, decorated with repoussé ornamentation. Consequently it has survived only in an extremely fragmentary condition, and so a reconstruction drawing has been shown. These 'Parade-Shields' were presumably funerary versions of more robust shields which were actually used in combat. The original diameter was something like 61 cm. Note the central handle and the four or five terminals attached by staples to the inside of the shield. These may have been for the attachment of straps which would enable the shield to be worn on the back when not in use.

the responsibilities of Roman citizenship (military service and payment of taxes) but did not allow office-holding or participation in elections at Rome.

Having thus strengthened her position, Rome established colonies in Campania and the Liris valley and in 326 entered into an alliance with Neapolis: all moves which angered the Samnites and precipitated the Second Samnite War. This began in 326 and was pursued for over twenty years, despite even the humiliating Roman defeat at the Caudine forks in 321 where a double consular army was captured by the Samnites. The war ended, however, in 304 with the Samnites ceding control of the Liris valley.

The Third Samnite War began in 298. In a final bid to secure their independence the Samnites organized a grand alliance of Samnites, Etruscans, Celts and Umbrians. The seriousness for Rome was obvious, but the Romans were able to defeat their enemies piecemeal, their most notable victories being against the Samnites and Gauls at Sentinum in 295 and Apulonia in 293. Defeat of the Samnite-led coalition, completed in 290, gave Rome effective control over all the native Italian peoples south of the Po valley. Now only the Greek coastal cities of South Italy remained free.

In 282 Rome sent a garrison to Thurii in response to a request for aid against her marauding Lucanian neighbours. The people of Tarantum regarded this as interference within their sphere of influence and appealed for aid to their fellow Greek, King Pyrrhus of Epirus. Pyrrhus landed in Italy in 280 and won two 'Pyrrhic' victories at Heraclea and Asculum but was finally defeated in 275 and forced to leave Italy. Rome's dominance was now beyond challenge.

For most of this period the literary sources at our disposal are of lamentable quality. Our principal sources are Livy and Dionysius of Halicarnassus, who both worked at Rome during the reign of the Emperor Augustus (31 BC–AD 14). In fact the ancient accounts of the history of Rome only become truly reliable when Pyrrhus comes onto the scene. The campaigns of Pyrrhus were described by earlier Greek historians, some of whom, like Pyrrhus' court historian Proxenos, and indeed Pyrrhus himself,

actually witnessed the events described. Thus the descriptions of the Roman army contained in surviving accounts of the war with Pyrrhus can be regarded as reliable. All information concerning the Roman army in particular, and Roman history in general, before this date is unreliable.

Rome only started to produce her own native historians towards the end of the third century. These are known to modern historians as the 'annalists'. The only reliable information they had available to draw on for the early history of Rome were lists of magistrates and treaties of alliance, otherwise they had to use mythology and oral tradition. Livy and Dionysius relied heavily on the 'annalists' and thus, though their works are unreliable as a whole, they occasionally contain 'nuggets' of information which seem to reflect accurate and genuine tradition. The task of the modern military historian is to sift out these nuggets from the slurry wherein they float. Needless to say, there is little which can be written on this period with absolute certainty.

Any study of the Roman army within this period falls naturally into three sections dealing with the pre-hoplite army, the hoplite army, and the manipular army.

Etruscan statuette of a warrior on a candelabrum from the 'Circolo del Tritone', Vetulonia, now in Florence. The decoration on the back of the shield indicates that the warrior carries a more robust version of the 'Etruscan Parade Shield' which was actually used in combat.

The fact that the warrior carries the shield suspended from his shoulders, presumably to allow him to throw his spear, shows that the attachments on the back of the 'Parade Shield' were designed for attachment to straps. He also carries a mace in his left hand.

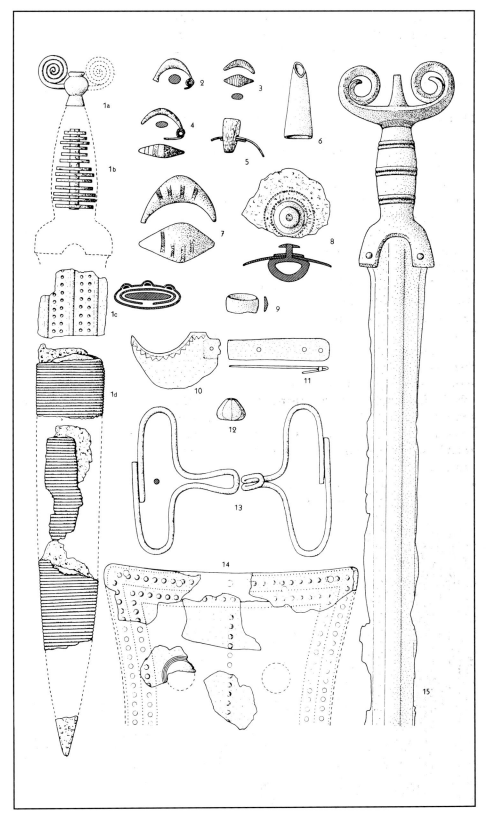

Left: This 'Calotte' helmet from Esquiline Tomb 94, now in the Capitoline Museum, has been dated to the first half of the seventh century. This early photograph demonstrates the fragmentary state of the skull: it is possible that the helmet originally had a number of plume and other fittings which were not recovered during excavation.

Findgroup 98 from the Esquiline, from a warrior-burial, excavated in the Via Giovanni Lanza. The short sword (1), found in a fragmentary condition, had an iron blade and a bronze pommel. The scabbard would have been wood, partially faced with an embossed bronze plate at top, and bound with a bronze wire. The bronze butt (6) has survived from the warrior's spear, but the iron spearhead had completely disappeared. The iron disk (8) may have been a boss from a wooden shield, though this is uncertain. The warrior's panoply was completed by a bronze pectoral (14) which also survived in a fragmentary state. Also shown are brooches (fibulae, 2–4, 7), used to secure the cloak and tunic, a bronze 'razor' or whittling-knife (10–11) and a belt-buckle (13).

THE PRE-HOPLITE ARMY

Traditionally Rome was founded in 753 BC by the twin brothers Romulus and Remus, sons of the god Mars, who had been suckled in infancy by a she-wolf. In fact the city of Rome first came into existence when separate communities on the Palatine and Quirinal hills amalgamated some time around 600 BC. The legend of Romulus and Remus only emerged during the fourth century under the influence of Greek writers. If there is any truth at all in the legend of the twins, one of whom had to die in order for a unified Roman people to emerge, it may be that two communities had to amalgamate to form Rome.

Warrior-burials on the Esquiline Hill

The earliest preserved remains from Rome date from the eighth and ninth centuries BC. At this time the huts of the village which would eventually become the Eternal City lay on the Capitoline Hill, while the necropolis of the settlement was situated on the Esquiline Hill. A number of early tombs there were excavated in 1885 during construction work on a

housing project. Of these tombs, some are clearly 'warrior-burials', while others contain assorted weapons. It is from these finds that we can form an image of the appearance of the earliest Roman warriors (see Plate A).

Only two helmets have emerged from early Rome, and both are of the 'Calotte' type, though it is possible that other helmet types were used too. The standard form of body-protection was the 'pectoral', or breastplate, of which some three have survived. They are rectangular in shape, with incurving sides, a little less than 20 cm wide and a little more than 20 cm long. Presumably they were worn with the long side running vertically, though this is not certain. The smaller sides are pierced with holes for the attachment of a leather backing and straps to hold the pectoral in place. The precise way in which these straps ran round the shoulders is unknown. The pectorals are decorated with bands of geometric ornamentation round the edge, and five bosses, one in the centre and one in each of the four corners.

One large ornamental bronze shield has survived. This shield is entirely Etruscan in style, and may well have been manufactured in one of the major manufacturing centres of Etruria, such as Tarquinii. We should also note, however, that an iron boss found separately might have come from a wooden shield. Two sizes of sword have been recovered, short swords about 44 cm long, and long swords about 70 cm long. The latter generally have an 'antenna' hilt. Sword blades at this time were generally bronze, but iron examples are occasionally found. Numerous spear-heads have been found in the Esquiline Tombs, sometimes of iron, sometimes of bronze. They have leaf-shaped blades and typically a multi-faceted central section, sometimes decorated with a geometric pattern.

Roman sardonyx gem showing two bearded Salii priests. (Photo: Staatliche Museen zu Berlin)

The Salii

Down to the end of the Republic and well into the Imperial period there existed at Rome two colleges of 'Salii', the priests of Mars. The cult of the *Salii Palatini* was connected with Mars and, according to tradition, with an ancient miraculous shield called an *ancile*. The *Salii Collini* was connected with Quirinus. Quirinus was the Sabine name for Mars, and was derived from the Sabine word for lance. Consequently we can be confident that two separate colleges of the Salii existed before the coalescence of the two separate communities on the Palatine and Quirinal hills around 600 BC. Many of the Republican institutions of Rome indicate that the early city incorporated both Latin and Sabine elements within its population.

Both colleges of priests were dedicated to the war-god, and many of the martial features of the institution of the Salii suggest that their origin lay in warrior bands bound by oath to serve the war-god. Each of the two colleges consisted of 12 life-members from patrician families, both of whose parents were required to be still living. This was presumably initially an injunction of military significance: the head of a family could not be a member of the Salii lest he should lose his life in battle. It may also indicate that at this early period the main social division between plebeian and patrician had military significance: only the patricians were rich enough to provide themselves with weapons, and were therefore able to participate in warfare. At the head of each college was a *magister*. The term *magister* is of military origin, denoting a magistracy or military command in Etruscan inscriptions.

It was a feature of most ancient communities that when new military or political institutions of the citizenry were established, they were placed under the protection of a particular deity. Worship was offered to the deity to ensure the survival and pros-

Below right: Raymond Bloch has suggested that this cornelian intaglio, present whereabouts unknown, shows two warriors rather than Salii, carrying five ancilia hung on a pole. The first warrior, however, seems to carry an apex in his hand. The seal dates to the fourth or third century BC; note the crested Italo-Attic helmets and muscle-cuirasses.

Right and below: Agate intaglio in the Archaeological Museum, Florence, showing two Salian priests moving the ancilia. It is inscribed, in Etruscan though the name is Latin, Appius alce 'Appius gave'.

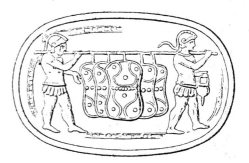

perity of that institution. In the course of time it would be necessary to reorganize the citizen body and establish new civic and military institutions. When this happened, however, the original institution frequently continued a shadowy existence as a social 'fossil', obsolete in any meaningful way, but continuing as a religious college which met to maintain the established acts of worship. Failure to maintain the established rites would constitute a sacrilegious act, and would be sure to bring down the wrath of the slighted god onto the community. In the priestly colleges of the Salii we seem to have such a fossil.

Some features of the institution of the Salii may therefore reflect Roman military practices before the institution of the tribal system. It may be that only young patricians participated in warfare, and only then if they were not heads of families. They formed themselves into warrior-bands, perhaps restricted to twelve men, who dedicated themselves to the worship of Mars in return for that god's support in battle. Needless to say, this is all highly speculative. Similar colleges of Salii existed in other Latin cities such as Aricia, Alba, Lavinium, Tusculum, Tibur and Anagnia. So this form of warfare seems to have been general in Latium, and not restricted to Rome.

Salian dress and equipment

The dress and equipment of the Salii are described by Livy, Dionysius of Halicarnassus and Plutarch. They wore a decorated many-coloured tunic, purple according to Plutarch, and what Livy calls 'a bronze covering for the chest'. These breastplates may correspond to the square pectorals recovered from the Esquiline tombs discussed above. Over the tunic was worn a *trabea* cloak described by Dionysius. His words are difficult to interpret, but he seems to say that they were striped in scarlet, bordered in purple and fastened with a brooch. Plutarch adds that they wore bronze belts and helmets and carried short daggers, while Dionysius tells us that they carried short spears or staffs.

The most distinctive item associated with the Salii was the *ancile*. The *ancile* was an oval shield made of bronze and decorated with relief work on the outside. The sides of these shields were indented. This rough 'figure-of-eight' shape has led to suggestions that the shield may have ultimately derived from Mycenaean prototypes, but the shape is so common in all areas at all times that a local Italian origin is to be preferred. No actual *ancilia* or shields of a comparable shape have survived, but small bronze votive shields of this shape have been recovered in archaeological contexts in Picenum and adjacent regions dating to 700 BC and later. Thus it seems possible to suggest that use of the *ancile* spread across the Apennines into Latium during the seventh century BC prior to the introduction of hoplite equipment and tactics. The actual origin of the *ancile*, as opposed to that in Roman tradition, is obscure. They may originally have been shields routinely used in battle by Roman warriors, or, less probably, booty captured from the enemy at some point in the past.

One further distinctive feature of the Salii was their pointed helmet, called an *apex*. An actual example of a Salian *apex* has been recovered in a late Republican context. It is made in silver, and so does not directly reflect an ancient helmet type, though it probably preserves an approximate representation of the shape of such an early helmet. Perhaps only the side ribs, brow-band and studs were metal in the

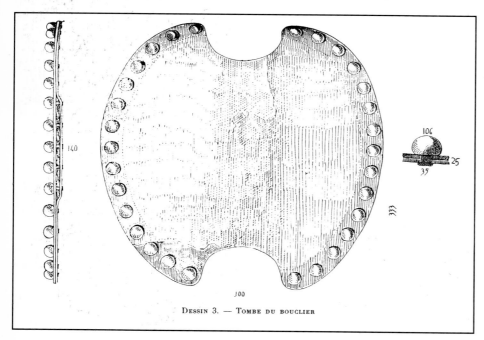

DESSIN 3. — TOMBE DU BOUCLIER

French archaeological excavations in the region of Bolsena revealed a warrior tomb, called by the excavator 'Tombe du Bouclier' after this bronze miniature (335×305 mm) shield, slightly oval in shape. The distinctive cut-out sections in the sides led the excavator to identify this type of shield as the ancestor of the ancilia *later carried by the Salii.*

14

original apex helmet, while the cap beneath them may have been leather. Perhaps the olive-wood spike at the top of the helmet may be the descendant of a wooden crest-holder.

The tribal system

The earliest possibly reliable information concerning the size and organization of the earliest Roman army describes how it was recruited from three 'tribes'. Roman society was at some early stage divided into three tribes and thirty *curiae*. The word *curia* is generally derived from *co-viria*, that is, 'an assembly of armed men'. The *curiae* formed the voting units of the earliest Roman assembly, the *comitia curiata*. Each *curia* was formed from a number of families (*gentes*) and ten of these *curiae* formed a tribe (*tribus*). That there were indeed originally three tribes is confirmed by the etymology of *tribus* which was derived from *tris* (the Latin for 'three') and literally meant 'divided into three'. Each tribe appears to have been commanded by a *tribunus militum* and to have contributed 1,000 men (i.e. 100 from each *curia*). This led the Roman antiquarian Varro to speculate that *miles* (the Latin for 'soldier')

The internal handle arrangements of the ancile are unknown. Hellenistic statues of Juno Sospita show handle arrangements similar to those for a hoplite shield, but they may have entered the representational canon under Greek influence, and perhaps do not represent seventh century reality. The inside of an ancile and an ornamental Salian dagger are shown on this example of a Roman aes grave coin, though such coins have been dismissed as forgeries.

was derived from *mille* (the Latin for 'a thousand'): 'soldiers are *milites* because at first the legion was made of three thousand and each of the individual tribes of Tities, Ramnes and Luceres sent a thousand soldiers'. Although Varro's etymology is probably incorrect (the true etymology of *miles* is unknown), the fact that he was able to suggest such an interpretation demonstrates that the tradition that each tribe contributed a thousand men to the legion was already well established when he wrote.

The horsemen in this organization are said to have been divided into three groups each of 100 men. Livy and Cicero tell us that these groups had the names Ramnes, Tities and Luceres, names which Varro said applied to the whole tribe. This should not worry us unduly – the longer survival of this early cavalry organization meant that these names were later associated only with the cavalry. It is unclear whether these cavalry are the same as the 300 *celeres* (literally 'the swift') who were supposedly instituted by Rome's first and legendary king, Romulus, as a bodyguard (*see* Livy, Festus, and Servius).

Exactly what these 'horsemen' were is obscure. True cavalry may not have existed at this time, and we can perhaps compare conditions in archaic Greece. Here the title of *hippeis* was given to élite

bands of hoplites who no longer used horses in battle but had originally used chariots, then horses, as a means of travelling to the battlefield and as an indication of their social status. Thus the Roman *equites* of the fifth century may have no more been horsemen than the Spartan *hippeis* of the same period.

Above: Silver apex helmet once belonging to one of the Salii, recovered from a water-reservoir beneath the atrium of the Domus Augustana on the Palatine. This presumably preserves the shape of a more practical archaic helmet, perhaps in leather with metal ribs and brim.

The principal emblem of the Flamen priest was his white pointed hat (apex) made from the hide of a sacrificed animal. The point was made of olive wood. The flamines were expected to wear this hat at all times when out of doors. This detail from the Ara Pacis Augustae shows two flamines wearing apex headgear.

Tradition claims that the tribal system was introduced by Romulus in the eighth century BC. But modern historians are unanimous in concluding that this cannot be the case. The three tribal names (Tities, Ramnes and Luceres) are clearly Etruscan. Consequently the system of three tribes and thirty *curiae* was introduced under the direct influence of the Etruscans, probably towards the end of the seventh century BC. This immediately raises the much larger problem of which method of warfare and equipment was used by the three tribes. It is possible that hoplite tactics and equipment were introduced at Rome at the same time as the tribal system, i.e. a little before 600 BC; but it is more probable that they were introduced some half-century later by Servius Tullius.

THE HOPLITE ARMY

Hoplite tactics were developed in Greece *c.* 675 BC and reached Etruria *c.* 600 BC, where their use is confirmed in a wide variety of contemporary artwork. Dionysius of Halicarnassus reports how the Etruscan towns of Falerii and Fescennium preserved hoplite equipment, despite being colonized by Romans: 'Falerii and Fescennium were even down to my day inhabited by Romans . . . in these cities there survived many ancient customs which the Greeks had once used, such as their type of weaponry: Argolic shields and spears'.

From Etruria this new form of warfare spread to Rome and to the other Latins. This fact is well established in the ancient tradition: 'In ancient times, when the Romans used rectangular shields, the Etruscans fought in phalanx using bronze shields, but having compelled the Romans to adopt the same equipment they were themselves defeated' (Diodorus). 'The Romans took close battle formation from the Etruscans, who used to attack in a phalanx' (Athenaeus). 'The Etruscans did not fight in maniples but made war on us armed with bronze shields in a phalanx; we were re-armed and adopting the equipment of the enemy we formed up against them; and in this way we were able to conquer even those most accustomed to fighting in phalanx' (*Ineditum Vaticanum*). Even Livy knew this, remarking that before the introduction of military pay the Romans had employed the round shield in a Macedonian style phalanx.

These two terracottas from Veii, produced at the beginning of the fifth century, show a pair of naked young men engaged in a war-dance. As in ancient Greece, the war dance was a survival of pre-hoplite warfare; its steps were designed to train the young warrior in the moves employed in single combat. One of the dancers carries a hoplite shield, while the other carries a square shield. The appearance of the square shield is difficult to interpret, but perhaps implies that when Rome was using hoplite methods of warfare not all other Latin cities followed suit, which is indicated in some literary sources. Both figurines would originally have had miniature spears in their right hands. (Photo: Museo Nazionale di Villa Giulia, Rome)

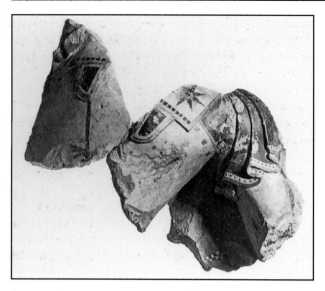

Painted terracotta body of an Amazon, dating to the early years of the fifth century, from the pediment of a temple on the Esquiline. The principal colour is sometimes stated to be black, but reproductions show a dark navy blue. It is by Greek artists, perhaps Damophilus and Gorgasus, known to have *been active in Rome at the same period. Clearly this sculpture is of a mythological subject, even though wearing hoplite equipment, and so cannot be taken as evidence for the adoption of hoplite equipment and even less so for hoplite tactics by the Roman army. (Photo: Soprintendenza Archeologica di Roma)*

The introduction of hoplite tactics to Rome is associated in Roman historical tradition with the penultimate king of Rome, Servius Tullius (traditional dates 578–534 BC). Servius was said to have introduced a sweeping reform which changed the prevailing social order divided by *gens* and *curia* which we have already described. The most important innovation was that citizenship by race was replaced by one based on residence, thus perhaps increasing the pool of military manpower. These newly defined citizens were subject to the *census* in which their wealth was assessed, and this in turn provided the basis for an army where the wealthy were bound to serve and to provide their own military equipment. Those obliged to serve armed as hoplites were said to be part of the *classis*; and those who were not sufficiently wealthy (perhaps the majority) were termed *infra classem* and may have served only as light armed troops (*see* Aulus Gellius, and Festus). That the *classis* was indeed a hoplite formation is confirmed by Festus who comments that

an army, known in his day as an *exercitus*, had in ancient times been called *classis clipeata* (i.e. the *classis* armed with the hoplite shield, *clipeus* being the Latin term for the hoplite shield).

A number of indications make it clear that the Servian political assembly, based on the division *classis: infra classem*, arose from a military reform. In later times the developed form of the citizen assembly still met outside the *pomerium* (the sacred boundary of the city of Rome) on the Campus Martius (a field dedicated to Mars, the Roman god of war); it could only be convened by a magistrate holding *imperium* (the authority required for military command); it was summoned by a trumpet blast (*classicum canere*) with red flags flying on the Janiculum and the Arx when assembled; and the formulae used to summon it included phrases like *exercitum imperare* (to command the army) and *exercitum urbanum convocare* (to summon the urban army). The inclusion of centuries of engineers and musicians also leads to the same conclusion. The fact that this 'Servian' system was entirely unsuitable for recruitment of a manipular army confirms its predominantly hoplite character, and it is hardly surprising that in creating this system Servius Tullius is thought to have introduced hoplite tactics to Rome.

Livy's account of the reforms

Anyone who reads the full historical accounts of early Rome written by Livy and Dionysius will note that they describe the 'Servian' reform somewhat differently from the simple division *classis: infra classem* outlined above. Livy's account (1.42.5–43.8) runs as follows:

'The population was divided into classes and centuries and the following arrangement, suitable for both peace and war, was made based upon the census. 1) Of those who had a census rating of 100,000 *asses* or more he made 80 centuries, 40 of seniors and 40 of juniors, all of whom were called the first Class. The seniors were to be ready to guard the city, and the juniors to wage war abroad. The armour which these had to provide consisted of helmet, round shield, greaves, and breast-plate (all of these items made of bronze), to protect the body; their offensive weapons were the spear and the sword. To this class were added two centuries of engineers who served without arms and whose duty was to construct siege engines in time of war. 2) The Second Class was drawn from those assessed between 75,000 and 100,000 *asses*, and from these 20 centuries (juniors and seniors) were formed. Their prescribed armour was the same as the first Class except for the breastplate and the rectangular shield in place of the round one. 3) He determined that the census rating of the third class should be 50,000 *asses*; the same number of centuries was made and the same arrangement by ages; nor was there any change in their arms except that greaves were omitted. 4) In the Fourth Class the census rating was 25,000 *asses*; the same number of centuries were formed but their equipment was changed: nothing was given them but a spear and a javelin. 5) The fifth Class was made larger with 30 centuries, and these carried slings with stones for missiles. Among this class were also the horn-blowers and trumpeters who were placed in two centuries. This class was assessed at 11,000 *asses*. 6) The lesser census rating contained all the rest of the population, and of these one century was formed which was exempt from military service.'

This account in Livy is largely paralleled in the description given by Dionysius in his *Roman Antiquities* (4.16.1–18.2). In Dionysius, however, the fourth class is equipped with shields, swords and spears where Livy gives just spears and javelins; and the fifth class are given javelins in addition to the slings in Livy. Dionysius adds the two centuries of artisans to the second class, not to the first class as in Livy, and he adds the centuries of musicians to the fourth class rather than to the fifth class. Finally he gives the census rating of the fifth class as a minimum of $12\frac{1}{2}$ *minae* (=12,500 *asses*) rather than 11,000 *asses* as in Livy. These are all minor differences, however, and in every other respect Dionysius' account is remarkably close to that in Livy.

The descriptions of the Servian army in Dionysius and Livy clearly assume that each of the census classes formed a line in the military formation. Thus the hoplites constituted the first line with

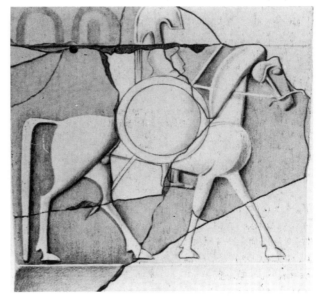

These moulded representations of mounted hoplites from Roman temples are likewise hardly evidence for the adoption of hoplite tactics by the Roman army, rather than simply hoplite equipment. Furthermore, many moulds used in Rome were also used in other towns in Latium and southern Etruria. Consequently we have no idea whether these moulds were even manufactured in Rome.

the second, third and fourth classes drawn up behind in that order, each with lighter equipment than the previous line. Finally the fifth class acted as skirmishers outside the line of battle. Such a formation contradicts our own description of the Servian army given above, an army composed entirely of hoplites all from a single *classis* supported perhaps by light armed from the *infra classem*. In this case we must examine the descriptions in Dionysius and Livy more closely and show why the five line multi-equipped army cannot truly represent conditions in sixth century BC Rome.

The Servian 40 century legion

This legion, drawn from an assembly with three distinctions of wealth, is itself a development from the original legion which, as we have seen, had only one census class. It is therefore most likely that in its earliest form the 'Servian' army consisted of just one class of hoplites and that classes II to V did not exist. The original Roman phalanx therefore consisted of one *classis* of 40 centuries of 'juniors' (i.e. 4,000 men) equipped in full hoplite panoply with light armed troops drawn from the *infra classem* who were not as yet organized into classes. At some point a further 20 centuries were added (i.e. classes II and III) to make the total 60 centuries. As the army organization expanded with the addition of the extra census classes, the original *classis* of forty centuries was preserved as the first class in the descriptions by Livy and Dionysius.

Fragments of a fictile plaque from the temple of Mater Matuta in Satricum, a town in Latium, showing an armoured warrior carrying a shield with a centaur blazon. Note the triangular plate to defend the groin suspended underneath the tunic. The sculpture dates to the late sixth or early fifth century. (Photo: Museo Nazionale di Villa Giulia, Rome)

The 60 century legion

What then is the correct chronology of the development from a legion drawn from a single hoplite class of 40 centuries to one of 60 centuries from an assembly divided into three census classes? Though we can offer no conclusive proof, the most appropriate time for this expansion seems to be the end of the fifth century BC. This was the time when Rome embarked on a ten year war with Veii (traditionally 406–396) which, when placed alongside the commitments generated by membership of the Latin League, must have greatly stretched her military resources. It was then that military pay was introduced for the first time (Livy), a development which looks very much like a measure intended to ease the burden on less wealthy citizens newly brought into the army.

The above analysis has attempted to outline what seems to be the most likely form of the 'Servian'

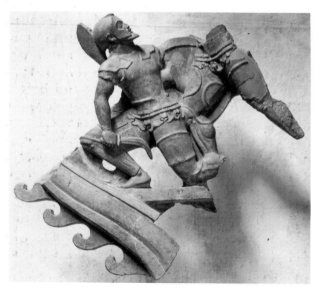

Fragment from the central acroterium of the Sassi Caduti temple at Falerii Veteres, showing an armoured warrior with a curved sabre. The use of auxiliary thigh and arm protectors died out in Greece in the sixth century, but they continued to be popular in Etruria. The sculpture dates to the beginning of the fifth century. (Photo: Museo Nazionale di Villa Giulia, Rome)

army up to the end of the fifth century BC. Given that the primary evidence is so scarce and so difficult to interpret, it is hardly surprising that other authors have adopted different approaches. We shall therefore also discuss alternative views.

Tradition assigns the adoption of hoplite tactics to the mid sixth-century BC, but there have been attempts to down-date the change to the mid-fifth century. M.P. Nilsson in particular argued that the hoplite reform occurred with the creation of the first military tribunes with consular power (444) and the creation of the censorship (443), but few historians now accept the link between the new offices and the census reform. A strong obstacle to Nilsson's view is the fact that the political assembly based on the 'Servian' reform was already in existence *circa* 450 BC and this implies an even earlier date for the army reform itself. Furthermore, it is very difficult to explain Rome's ability to hold her own in a world dominated by Etruscan military power and even to carve for herself a significant hegemony in Latium if she had not adopted the most advanced military practices of the day. It seems an inescapable conclusion therefore that Rome did not lag far behind in copying her neighbours.

Fifth century terracotta from Veii showing Aeneas carrying Anchises. This terracotta is of principal interest as early archaeological evidence for the legend of the Trojan migration to Latium. It is also of interest as one of the earliest representations from Latium of a warrior wearing a short tunic and equipped with greaves, a muscle-cuirass and a crested Italo-Attic helmet. This combination becomes almost standard for all Latin hoplites. (Photo: Museo Nazionale di Villa Giulia, Rome, Inv. no. 40272)

Nilsson did, however, draw attention to one piece of evidence for the use of hoplite tactics. This is the incident recorded under 432 BC when the dictator Aulus Postumius had his son executed for leaping out of the battle-line to engage the enemy single handed. A similar event is recorded under 340 BC when the consul T. Manlius Torquatus was said to have executed his son for the same offence (both in Livy). No wonder that elsewhere in Livy's narrative individuals are especially concerned to get permission before engaging in single combat! Whether these reports are genuine is debatable, especially as far as the accuracy of the dates is concerned, but they may conceivably be recollections of the sort of military discipline especially appropriate to the phalanx. We should note, however, that these reports do not help us date the introduction of the phalanx – hoplite warfare could have had a long history even in 432 BC and our mid sixth century BC date must stand. (On this phenomenon see S.P. Oakley, 'Single Combat in the Roman Republic', *Classical Quarterly* 35 (1985) 392–410.)

We have argued above that the hoplite army created by Servius Tullius had a strength of 4,000 and was later augmented to 6,000 at the end of the fifth century BC. Others (though far from all) have suggested that the 60 century army was itself the direct result of Servius' reform and not a later development. That the original Servian army had 60 centuries seems unacceptable because it rejects the relevance of the distinction *classis: infra classem* in favour of less satisfactory evidence. The evidence for the 60 century army is merely that in the descriptions given by Livy and Dionysius the equipment assigned to the first three classes (i.e. the first 60 centuries of 'juniors') belongs to various forms of heavy infantry while that given to classes IV and V is much lighter. But along with many other modern historians the present writers believe that the descriptions in Dionysius and Livy are not based on genuine knowledge of archaic conditions, but are the result of quite arbitrary antiquarian reconstruction, and cannot therefore be pressed as evidence. Furthermore, the assignment of light equipment to the centuries of classes IV and V is bogus because we have no genuine evidence for the light armed ever being organized into centuries (this was certainly not the case in the manipular army).

A more acceptable variant on this interpretation is that, although the army instituted by Servius consisted of 40 centuries, it expanded quickly to a total of 60 centuries by the beginning of the Republic (trad. 509 BC). The difference with the present interpretation is one merely of timing. We prefer to think that the expansion better fits conditions *c*. 400 BC. Those who pursue the theory of an earlier expansion argue that at the beginning of the republic the army was split into two legions, one for each of the two consuls. This is of course possible, but we should note that there is no positive evidence for this and that the proposition relies entirely on intuition. We shall discuss the question of the increase in the number of legions in further detail below.

Our conclusion from all this has three parts. Hoplite tactics were introduced into Rome, via Etruria, in the mid sixth century BC. The earliest Roman hoplite army was composed of 40 centuries of hoplites. At some point before the creation of an additional legion the 40 centuries were augmented by the addition of a further 20 centuries. Some suggest that this took place before the collapse of the Roman monarchy (trad. 509 BC) but the present authors prefer *c*. 400 BC as a more likely date.

EARLY CAVALRY

The sex suffragia

It should come as no surprise that, just as with the centuries of infantry, the Servian cavalry organization described by Livy and Dionysius is not genuinely archaic. Livy describes how Servius added twelve centuries to the pre-existing cavalry force of six centuries:

'So with the infantry force armed and organized in this way, 12 centuries of cavalry were enrolled from among the leading men of the state. He formed a further six centuries (three had been created by Romulus) with the same traditional names. For the purchase of horses 10,000 *asses* were given from the state treasury, and for their upkeep rich widows were assigned to pay 2,000 *asses* each year.'

The six centuries to which Servius is supposed to have added his twelve were titled Tities *priores* and *posteriores*, Ramnes *priores* and *posteriores*, and Luceres *priores* and *posteriores*. In later times these six centuries had a special status and were known as the *sex suffragia* ('the six votes'), a title which distinguished them from the remaining twelve equestrian centuries in the *comitia centuriata* (Livy, Cicero, Festus 452L). It is almost certain therefore that there had once been only six centuries of *equites* and that the addition of a further twelve could not have been the work of Servius Tullius. The error made by Roman historians was to assume that the final total of 1,800 *equites* in the late republic was not the product of a later increase in their numbers (for which see below) but had been instituted at the very beginning by Servius. Furthermore, they did not realize that 1,800 is an impossibly high figure for the cavalry resources of archaic Rome.

It would seem superficially obvious that the *sex suffragia* of *equites* reflects an original force of 600 cavalry, but a significant problem here is that we have no evidence of cavalry in later times being organized into centuries as was the infantry. Later Roman cavalry were organized into *turmae* of 30 men, each

Italian muscle-cuirass. This example, in the British Museum, is from Ruvo in South Italy and dates to the second half of the fourth century. Italian muscle-cuirasses can be easily distinguished from Greek examples as they have no shoulder-guards. (Photo: N.V. Sekunda)

divided into three *decuriae* of ten men. Indeed the ancient religious ceremony known as the *transvectio equitum*, which was probably instituted in the early fifth century BC, was performed by six *turmae* and not six centuries.

The retention of the titles Tities, Ramnes and Luceres suggests that the Servian reform itself did not fundamentally alter the organization or recruitment of the Roman *equites*. They remained drawn from the three tribes and there seems to have been no special census rating for service as an *eques* over and above that of the infantry. Livy states merely that they were drawn from the 'leading men of the state' (*ex primioribus civitatis*).

These considerations combine to suggest that the *sex suffragia* were not six centuries of true cavalry. It seems that the three tribal centuries of *equites* survived the Servian reform as an élite hoplite band, not as true cavalry, and assumed the honorific title of centuries *priores*. The date and circumstances of the addition of the three centuries of Tities, Ramnes and Luceres *posteriores* are quite obscure. Perhaps an expansion in the 'leading men of the state' dictated an expansion in the number of equestrian centuries. Whether this occurred at the time of the Servian reform or at a later date is uncertain.

The designations *priores* and *posteriores* suggest not only a notional position in the battle-line. Greek cavalrymen would be individually attended by mounted grooms who would withdraw behind the cavalry when the troops were formed up. Perhaps the *equites posteriores* fulfilled a theoretical relationship of grooms to the *equites priores*; and it may be that this notional doubling suggested to the antiquarians that at some stage the *priores* had made use of two horses. Interesting details have been preserved by Granius Licinianus and Festus concerning the supply of two horses to some of the cavalry: 'The Romans used the same number of horses, that is two, in battle so that they might transfer to a fresh one when the other was worn out; the double amount given to the cavalrymen for two horses was called the *aes pararium*' (Festus); 'I shall not pass over the cavalry which Tarquin introduced in such a way that the centuries of *priores* led two horses into battle' (Granius Licinianus).

The public horse and true cavalry

The first plausible evidence for the establishment of a force of true cavalry at Rome comes in 403 BC: during the final and decisive struggle with Veii. As has already been noted, this war saw the introduction of military pay and probably also the expansion of the infantry Legion. Livy records that 403 was the first year in which cavalrymen served on their own horses and that they were then rewarded by the introduction of pay for the cavalry. Such volunteers serving on their own mounts were called *equites equo privato* or *equites suis merentes*.

How funds were raised to provide this pay is unknown. In the later Republic Rome also main-

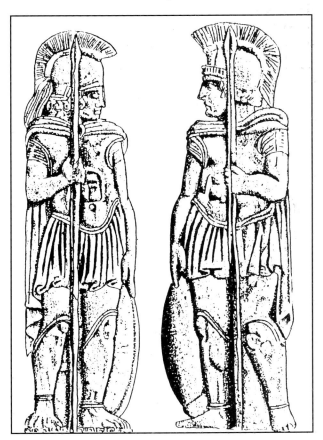

These two bone plaques from Palestrina, dating to the fourth century, belong to a series of laminae of different sizes, which probably once formed the veneer of a magistrate's seat of office (sella curulis). This pair of hoplite warriors wear the dress and equipment typical of Latin hoplites of the period: crested Italo-Attic helmets, muscle-cuirasses, and greaves, together with a short tunic and cloak. Note the round clasps securing the cloak. (Photo: Museo Nazionale di Villa Giulia, Rome, Inv. nos. 13236, 13237. Courtesy Montvert Publications)

Front and back views of the handle of a lid of a Praenestine cist showing two warriors carrying the body of a third home. This cista is one of the earlier ones in the series and probably dates to the end of the fourth century. Unlike the overwhelming majority of depictions of hoplites from Latium they do not wear greaves, and they wear the composite cuirass instead of the muscle-cuirass. The muscle-cuirass may not have been universal in Latium at this period, or perhaps Etruscan hoplites are meant to be shown. (Photo: Museo Nazionale di Villa Giulia, Rome, Inv. 25210)

tained another force of cavalry whose mounts were provided at public expense, and who were paid an allowance for fodder. These cavalry were called *equites equo publico*. It is not known whether the institution of *equites equo publico* existed before the establishment of the *equites equo privato* in 406 BC, but this seems highly unlikely as raising the resources to supply horses and fodder required much more strenuous fiscal effort than simply providing cavalry pay. Consequently we are drawn to the conclusion that prior to 406 BC the title *eques* was purely honorific.

In contemporary Sparta and Corinth the provision of horses for the cavalry was a fiscal requirement imposed on the estates of widows and orphans, which were administered by the state upon the death of the head of a household. Livy records the imposition by Servius of taxes on orphans and widows, but the *aes equestre* (the tax to provide horses) and the *aes hordearium* (the tax to provide fodder) were probably later developments which have been incorrectly attributed to Servius. In a different strand of the Roman historical tradition to that in Livy, we find the introduction of similar taxes attributed to M. Furius Camillus in 403, this time on unmarried men and orphans (Plutarch and Valerius Maximus). It is possible therefore that the institution of *equites equo publico* was established then.

We presume that the original *equites equo privato* were by and large recruited from the 'leading citizens' of the *sex suffragia* (by this time a political grouping rather than a military organisation), and the establishment of the *equites equo publico* enabled all 600 to serve as cavalry. The expansion of the *equites equo publico* to a strength of 1,800 probably only occurred towards the end of the fourth century BC (*see* below). In the Second Punic War, when the number of *equites equo publico* was insufficient to provide the cavalry complement of a vastly increased number of legions, the institution of *equites equo privato* had to be relied on once again.

As has already been mentioned, tradition maintained that before the Servian Reform three tribal centuries of *equites* had existed, but it is doubtful whether these 'horsemen' ever operated as true cavalry on the hoplite battlefield. In Archaic Greece forces of true cavalry were only maintained by Thessaly and Boeotia. In these two states there existed an aristocracy sufficiently wealthy and powerful to provide their own cavalry horses. Elsewhere Athens had created a force of 300 cavalry by 457, later expanded to 1,200 *circa* 443; Sparta created a force of 400 cavalry in 424, and few other Greek states had any force of cavalry worth mentioning before the closing decades of the fifth century BC.

The principal reason for the late emergence of cavalry in Greece was the difficulty in providing horses, or compensation for privately owned horses killed in battle, and allowances for fodder. Before the invention of the horse collar in the medieval period oxen were used to plough and to pull carts, and the horse was simply used as an extravagant means of transport. Aristocrats with the wealth to maintain horses were few and were reluctant to gamble their expensive pets on the battlefield. Like the hoplite city-states of Greece, the hoplite city-states of Italy needed to develop methods of raising state revenues before they could subsidize and compensate horse-owning aristocrats for their service as cavalrymen. Consequently it is unlikely that Rome possessed any true force of cavalry before the last decades of the fifth century BC.

THE EXPANSION OF ROMAN MILITARY STRENGTH

By the end of the fourth century BC the Roman army definitely comprised four legions. Unfortunately there is no specific ancient testimony telling us exactly when and how new legions came into being. Instead we have to proceed using a mixture of guess-work, assessment of probabilities, and inference. The type of problem confronting us should be clear when we recognize that an increase in the number of Roman legions could be the result of two quite different processes. On the one hand, existing man-power could have been split into a larger number of units (i.e. a purely organizational development involving no increase in manpower). On the other it could be the case that new units were created by means of increased conscription. It is quite possible, moreover, that both processes operated at different stages of development. What follows is an outline of the most likely pattern of development in the fourth century BC.

The infantry

We have already attempted to show that the Roman army *c.* 400 consisted of a single legion of 6,000 men. In 366, however, after many years of electing military tribunes with consular power as the main officers of state, Rome resumed the election of just two annual consuls. It is likely that it was as a response to this that the legion was split into two. At this time Rome cannot have been in a position to recruit extra troops from thin air; manpower must therefore have remained the same and was now divided into two

Scene from the painted frescoes of the François Tomb from Vulci. Dating from the second half of the fourth century, the tomb shows both mythological and historical scenes. In this historical scene the Etruscan Aule Vipinas (Latin Aulus Vibenna) kills one Venthi Cau[ ]plsachs, *possibly a Faliscan rather than a Roman, but a Latin for sure. He is equipped with hoplite shield, muscle-cuirass and greaves, and dressed in the short tunic we have seen to be typical of Latin hoplites at this period. The tunic colour is red.*

This Praenestine cist has not been firmly dated yet, but the equipment shown indicates a date on the eve of the adoption of manipular weapons and tactics in Latium. The traditional hoplite shield and spear, the muscle-cuirass, greaves, tunic and cloak are retained unchanged, but the Italo-Attic helmet has been replaced with helmets of the Montefortino type. (Photo: Hermitage, St Petersburg, Inv. B 619)

legions each of 3,000 men. We know from Livy, however, that by 311 Rome had four legions. He comments that this year saw 'the election by the people of sixteen military tribunes for distribution amongst the four legions, whereas these had previously been almost exclusively in the gift of the dictators and consuls' and the implication is that the existence of four legions was a recent development. These legions were undoubtedly formations organized around the maniple and, if we follow Polybius' description of the manipular legion, consisted of 3,000 heavy infantry and 1,200 light-armed. The total force was therefore 12,000 heavy infantry and 4,800 light troops: more than double that available in 366.

Such a large increase becomes understandable when we consider Rome's successes in the fourth century BC, particularly her defeat of the Latins and the conditions of the peace made in 338. Rome imposed terms on her defeated enemies which significantly increased the pool of citizen manpower. Not only were the towns of Lanuvium, Aricia, Nomentum, Pedum, Velitrae and Antium all given full Roman citizenship; but a new type of citizenship was also introduced. This was the *civitas sine suffragio* (citizenship without the vote), a status whereby the holder was liable for taxation and military service but could not participate in Roman political assemblies or hold office. This *civitas sine suffragio* was given to the important Campanian towns of Capua, Suessula and Cumae (plus Acerrae in 332), and the Volscian towns of Fundi and Formiae (and Privernum in 329).

These grants in themselves hugely increased available manpower, but Rome pursued another policy which must also have had the same effect. This was the appropriation of some of the land of a number of defeated opponents. Land confiscation allowed the settlement of Roman citizens – citizens who previously may have been too poor to be liable to military service under the 'Servian' system. But now, with their new land, they would become sufficiently wealthy to qualify for military service.

Thus even without the creation of *civitas sine suffragio* Rome would probably have increased her available manpower. But with all these measures combined, the increase must have been colossal. The census records for the fourth century BC are generally considered to be very unreliable, and we are therefore unable to quantify this increase precisely, but we can at least note that because of the expansion of the mid fourth century BC the area of land occupied by Roman citizens increased from *circa* 1,500 square kilometres to *circa* 5,500. And we should not forget that allied communities possessing treaties with Rome also had to supply their own contingents for Rome's wars.

It should therefore cause us no surprise that sometime between 338 and 311 Rome was able to double her infantry force to four legions.

Legionary blazons

From the evidence given above it seems that at some date after 338 BC the Roman army comprised four legions, and for a number of years before manipular equipment and tactics were introduced these legions may have been equipped as hoplites. Pliny, after telling us that Marius gave the Roman legions their eagle standards during his second consulship in 104 BC, mentions that previously the legions carried eagle standards as their first badge, but that in addition they carried four others; wolves, minotaurs, horses and boars going in front of the various *ordines*. *Ordo* usually means 'rank' and so the natural interpretation of Pliny's words would be that these standards would be carried in front of the various ranks of the manipular army: that is the *triarii*, *principes* and *hastati*. There is an obvious problem that four standards do not go into three ranks, so it seems reasonable to assume that Pliny has misunderstood his source, presumably one of the 'antiquarians'. Given that there were traditionally four legions from the closing decades of the fourth century onwards, it is tempting to assume that Pliny's source was describing the four legionary standards.

Two of the four legions would have been the two Roman legions most probably formed after the legionary split in 366 BC. For these two 'Roman' legions the devices of the wolf and the boar would be the most appropriate symbols. The wolf, together with the woodpecker, was the animal sacred to Mars (Plutarch, *Life of Romulus* 4). We have already met the she-wolf, sacred to Mars, in the legend of Romulus and Remus, which was already reaching its finished form during the fourth century. The wolf does not appear by itself as a symbol in Roman republican coinage, but the she-wolf suckling Romulus and Remus does, and it is tempting to assume that this is the symbol (perhaps of *Legio I*)

Following the extension of citizenship to the Campanians, the human-faced bull starts to appear on Roman coins. This half or quarter litra, showing the protome of a human-headed bull on its reverse, was issued c. 300 BC. (Photo: Hirmer Fotoarchiv, München)

Coin struck in Neapolis by the Campanian League circa 340 BC, bearing the device of a human-faced bull, presumably the badge of the Campanian people as a whole. The same device occurs on coins of other Campanian cities, such as Cales and Hyria, as well as on coins of Rome itself.

which Pliny's source is describing. The significance of the boar is less certain. We might note that in Imperial times the boar was one of the symbols of the *Legio X Fretensis* and the symbol of the *Legio XX Valeria Victrix*. Its significance has not been explained so far, but it was perhaps originally the symbol of Quirinus, the Sabine equivalent of Mars, who had continued to have a separate cult existence in Rome after the amalgamation of the two founding communities around 600 BC.

The symbols of horse and minotaur are even more difficult to explain. However, they may allude to the origins of the two new legions. In Greek iconography the minotaur is shown as a bull-headed human, and, indeed, such a beast is shown on an early moulded relief from Rome. The human-headed bull is, however, much more common, especially on Sicilian and Italian coins, where it is usually interpreted as representing some or other river-god. The human-headed bull was also the symbol of the Campanians. This is presumably the minotaur referred to by Pliny's source. Thus it may be suggested that one of the four legions of the late fourth century was formed from Campanians to whom Roman citizenship had been extended, hence they took as their badge the former national symbol of Campania.

The horse cannot be explained in a similar way, as it appears on Italian coins issued by a large number of towns. Thus it cannot be isolated as the symbol of a particular region. We note, however, that citizenship was extended to both Latin and Volscian communities at about the same time as it was to the Campanians, and it may be that these communities made up the fourth legion. On Roman republican coins the horse frequently appears as a device on those which bear the head of Mars on the obverse.

The cavalry

We have already suggested that the Roman army of the very late fifth century BC had a maximum of six centuries of cavalry, and that these were represented in the electoral assembly by the *sex suffragia*. We have also seen that the further twelve centuries of the electoral assembly which brought the total up to eighteen were a later addition. It is interesting therefore that the twelve additional centuries amount to the total cavalry component of a four legion manipular army (*see* Polybius). It seems very likely therefore that the introduction of the four legion army was accompanied by an overhaul of the cavalry in which 1,200 new *equites equo publico* were created, 300 per legion. The existing force represented in the *sex suffragia* must have been relegated to a ceremonial and electoral role only. A hint of this large increase in cavalry resources can be found in the *Ineditum Vaticanum* whose author stressed Rome's need greatly to augment her cavalry forces in order to face the Samnites (quoted below).

Etruscan Mirror, dating to the late fourth century or early third century. In Etruscan iconology, influenced by the struggle against Roman expansion, it is normal for Etruscans to be represented as Greeks and Romans as Trojans. This arose out of the commonly held belief that the Roman nation grew from Trojan immigrants originally settled in Latium by Aeneas. By extension it could be argued that on this mirror Hercules (Herkle) represents an Etruscan while the Amazon Hephleta represents a Roman. As a shield blazon Hephleta has the head of a human-headed bull: perhaps a Roman legionary shield blazon. The martial goddess Minerva looks on.

The Earliest Roman Warriors,
c.700 BC
1: 'Romulus'
2: 'Remus'

A

Roman Warrior Bands, seventh century BC   1: Salian warrior   2: Flamen priest

B

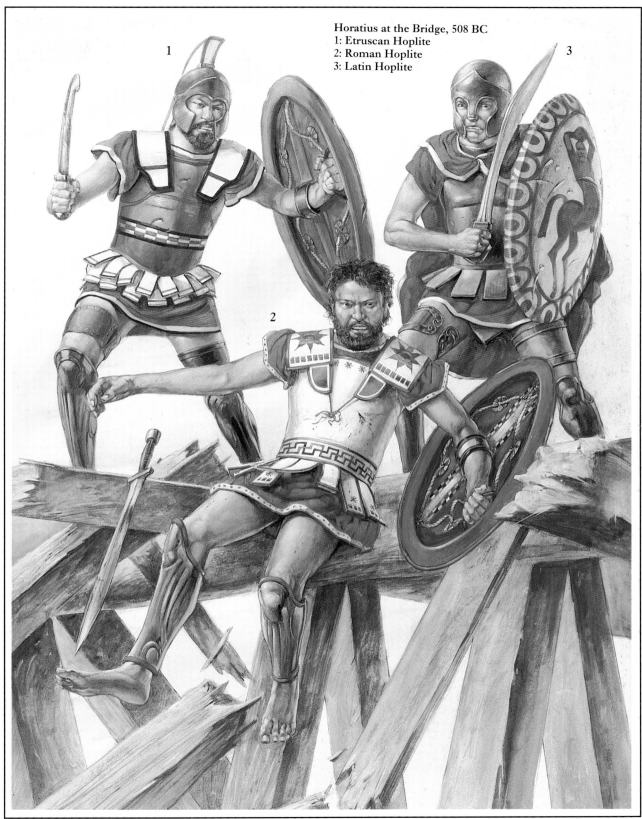

Horatius at the Bridge, 508 BC
1: Etruscan Hoplite
2: Roman Hoplite
3: Latin Hoplite

C

The Venetic Fighting System, fifth century BC
1: Pikeman
2: Shield-bearer
3: Hoplite
4: Axe-man

D

Roman Hoplites defeated by Celts, fourth century BC
1, 2, 3: Roman Hoplites
4: Celtic horseman
5: Celtic swordsman

E

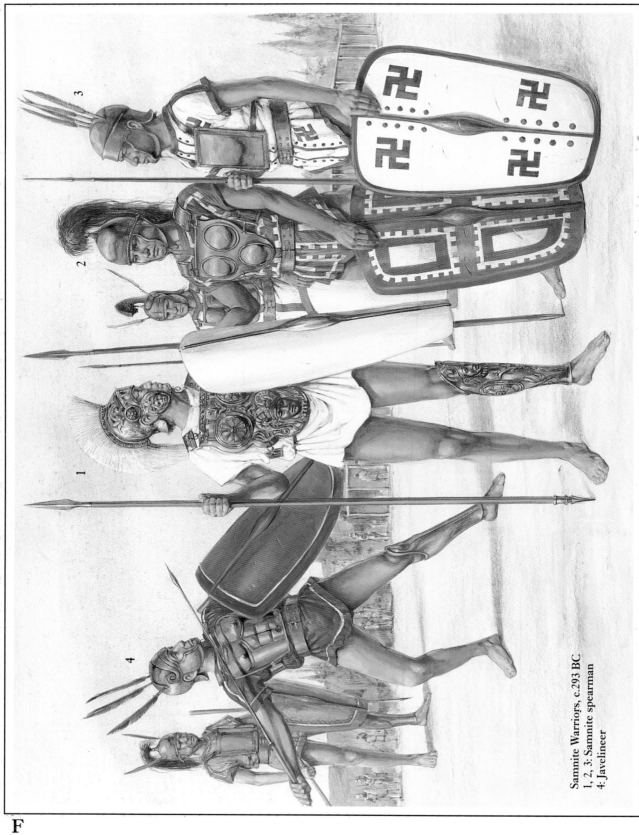

Samnite Warriors, c.293 BC
1, 2, 3: Samnite spearman
4: Javelineer

F

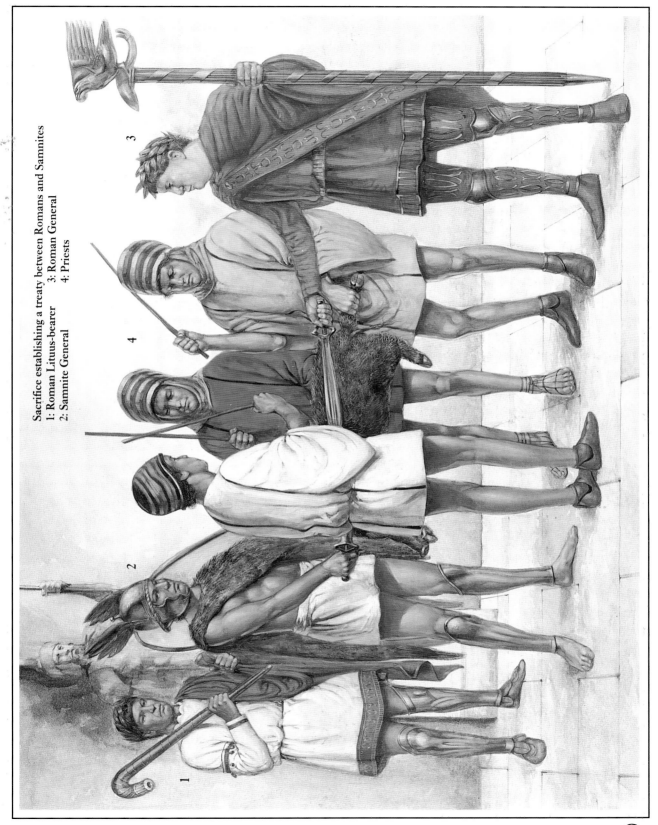

Sacrifice establishing a treaty between Romans and Samnites
1: Roman Lituus-bearer   3: Roman General
2: Samnite General   4: Priests

G

Roman Hastati fight one
of Pyrrhus' elephants
1: Roman Hastati
2: Epirote war elephant

H

The expansion of the strength of the *equites equo publico* to 1,800 seems not to have been the only increase in Roman cavalry resources. In 340 1,600 Capuan *equites* were granted Roman citizenship for their loyalty to Rome at a time when the rest of Capua had deserted to Rome's enemies. In addition the Capuans were forced to provide each cavalryman with 450 *denarii* to pay for the upkeep of their horses (Livy).

MANIPULAR WARFARE

Whilst hoplite warfare remained dominant from the middle of the sixth century BC down through the fourth in Latium and many areas of Italy, elsewhere in the peninsula other forms of warfare were ascendant. Eventually one of these, manipular warfare, was adopted by the Roman legions. legions. Essentially the manipular formation consisted of a number of lines of infantry, each line consisting of blocks of troops (maniples) with wide spaces separating the maniples, enabling them to advance or withdraw independently of the movement of the battle-line as a whole. Each line of maniples might be equipped differently.

At some point during the fourth century BC the Roman hoplite phalanx was abandoned and replaced by the much more flexible 'manipular' formation. When and why this took place are obvious questions, but they are not so easily answered.

The Gallic invasions

Many have stressed the importance of the defeat at the Allia at the hands of the Gauls, and have claimed that this disaster led the Romans to adopt the manipular formation. Dionysius and Plutarch certainly believed that some form of tactical change was employed when the Gauls next returned. Both claim that it was under the guidance of M. Furius Camillus that the Romans adopted the oval shield (*scutum*) and the heavy javelin (*pilum*) to replace the round shield (*clipeus*) and the thrusting spear (*hasta*) of the hoplites. Neither author explicitly records the introduction of maniples, but this must be assumed since the adoption of these weapons without the appropriate manipular formation would be a nonsense.

Dionysius tells how the Roman soldiers ducked down under the blows of the Gallic swords and took them on the shield, while striking at the enemies' groin with the sword. Plutarch gives a slightly different variation, saying oddly that the Gallic blows were taken on the *pilum*, but we should treat such descriptions with great caution. We know, for instance, that a different sort of tactic had been employed much later in defeating the Gauls at Telamon in 225 BC. Here the first Roman line was equipped with the *hasta* instead of the *pilum* and the *hastae* were used to take the initial blows of the enemy. It seems difficult therefore to believe that earlier Romans, as according to Plutarch at least, had defeated the Gauls by doing precisely the opposite and abandoning the *hasta*. What seems to have happened is that these late authors knew that the Gauls had been defeated and

European shields of the late Bronze Age and early Iron Age frequently have either 'U-notch' or 'V-notch' decoration. Such shields are called Herzsprung shields after the site where the principal shield in the series was found. This example of a 'U-notch' shield from Bohemia is closest to the shields shown on the Certosa Situla, even though it is much earlier in date. (Photo: J. Coles)

Reconstruction of the Certosa Situla. The uppermost register shows the four groups of Infantrymen discussed in the text. (after P. Ducati, La Situla della Certosa, 1923)

assumed that some tactical innovation must have been employed. With this in mind they gave a garbled and unlikely version (for which they probably had no direct evidence) of later tactics.

There is a further and a stronger argument against the Gauls acting as the catalyst for the introduction of manipular tactics and equipment at Rome. The Romans will presumably have copied manipular tactics from an enemy who had shown this formation to be superior to the phalanx. This enemy could hardly have been the Gauls since they certainly did not use manipular tactics. The origins of manipular warfare are obscure, and the existing literary fragments shed no light on the question. The earliest possible depiction of manipular warfare comes on an object known as the Certosa Situla.

The Certosa Situla

The situla is decorated with four registers showing an animal scene, a banqueting scene, a sacrificial procession and a parade of warriors. It is the parade with which we are principally concerned. The parade opens with two cavalrymen dressed in a fringed tunic, covered by what appears to be some kind of cuirass made out of coarsely-woven thick textile material, and pot helmet. They carry palstave axes over the shoulder. It is possible that the two horsemen represent an illustrative attempt to indicate that the infantry line was supported by cavalry stationed on either flank. The horsemen are then followed by one group of five infantrymen, and then by three other groups of four. The warriors of each group are identically equipped, but each group is different.

The first group of warriors carry long oval shields. The shields have a narrow border and in the centre a boss of 'Herzsprung' shape. The fringed hem of a tunic is shown beneath the shield on some of the figures, and it is possible that a textile cuirass, similar to that worn by the horsemen, would have been worn behind the shield. The spear is considerably longer than those carried by the other figures on the situla, and it ends in a long butt-spike. The warriors wear a 'disk and stud' helmet. The helmet is held on by a strap passing under the chin. When these and other figures from the Certosa Situla are illustrated, the photographs show the cheeks of these warriors represented by bulges punched out of the bronze sheeting. These should not be interpreted as metal disks attached to the chin strap.

The second group of infantrymen carry square shields with rounded edges and a square boss at the centre. The third group of warriors carry round shields with rims decorated with a triangular pattern. As the shields of both these groups of warriors reach almost to the knee, we are unable to see whether they wear tunics or any body armour. Both groups wear pot helmets and carry hoplite spears with quite wide leaf-shaped points. All three groups of spearmen carry their spears reversed, with the points towards the ground. This may represent standard battlefield practice during the advance, or it could have funerary significance.

It could be suggested that these groups of spearmen are intended to represent a manipular battle-line in two dimensions, and are thus ancestors of the Roman *acies triplex* of *hastati*, *principes* and *triarii*. Unlike the Roman battle-line, however, the Venetic warriors all carry fighting spears rather than javelins. Other examples of Veneto-Illyrian bronze work, such as the Arnoaldi situla, show warriors

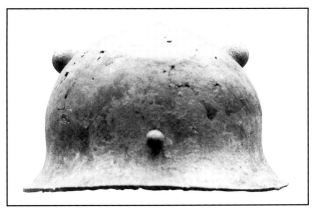

with oblong shields, helmets and a pair of javelins, and the Carpena decorated plaque shows warriors with round shields, helmets and a pair of javelins. Such troops would use armament much more appropriate for precursors of Roman *manipularii*, and it may be, indeed, that this type of weaponry gradually replaced that shown on the Certosa Situla.

Behind the three groups of spearmen march a final group of four unshielded infantrymen, wearing fringed tunics, textile cuirasses like those worn by the cavalrymen and conical helmets and carrying palstave axes over their shoulders. What are these figures supposed to represent? In the Roman manipular battle line the light infantry commenced the fight by engaging the enemy with javelins before the two battle-lines closed. When this happened the light infantry withdrew through the gaps between the maniples and re-formed behind the third line. These Venetic axe men may also be light infantry. On the other hand the battlefield role of the axemen may have been to finish off enemy wounded as the triple battle-line advanced. Conical helmets of similar type are also shown on other pieces of bronze-work produced by the Veneto-Illyrian culture.

Whatever the validity of these varied speculations may be in detail, it certainly does seem that in the Certosa Situla we can see a representation of a precursor of the manipular tactics which would even-

Above: Bronze Italian pot-helmet, once crested, found near Ancona in the Picenum and now in the British Museum. These pot-helmets remained popular within the Picene and adjacent regions much later than in other areas of Italy. The resemblance between this helmet and those shown on the Certosa Situla is obvious. (Photo: N.V. Sekunda)

This example of a 'Disc and stud' helmet is similar to those worn by the first group of warriors on the Certosa Situla. It is from Slovenia, within the Venetic-Illyrian cultural region. (Photo: Narodni muzej, Ljubljana)

tually spread to Rome at the end of the fourth century BC. It should be noted, however, that the varied and multiple battle-line which is shown on the Certosa Situla is not repeated on other surviving examples of decorated bronze-work left by the Veneto-Illyrian culture showing military scenes.

Samnite warfare

Since the Gauls did not cause the Romans to change their formation and weapons it is almost certain that the Samnites were responsible. Indeed this was believed by some ancient authors. Athenaeus wrote that 'they learned the use of the *scutum* from the Samnites'; Sallust said that 'our ancestors . . . took their offensive and defensive weapons from the Samnites'; and the author of the *Ineditum Vaticanum* wrote: 'We did not have the traditional Samnite *scutum* nor did we have the *pilum*. But we fought with round shields and spears; nor were we strong in cavalry either but all or the greater part of the Roman army was infantry. But when we became involved in a war with the Samnites we were equipped with the *scutum* and the *pilum* and had forced ourselves to fight as cavalry; so with foreign weapons and copied tactics we enslaved those who had developed a conceited pride in themselves.'

The explanation is clear. In their wars against the Samnites over the rough terrain of central southern Italy the hoplite phalanx proved to be much less effective than the more flexible formation used by the Samnites. The latter employed a large number of smaller and more manoeuvrable units (maniples) of soldiers equipped with heavy javelins and the *scutum*.

Fortunately two passages in Livy contain much valuable information on the dress, equipment and organization of the Samnite army during the last two Samnite Wars. This information is frequently dismissed as extremely untrustworthy by modern historians. In what follows, however, we have assumed that what Livy tells us, although distorted, especially

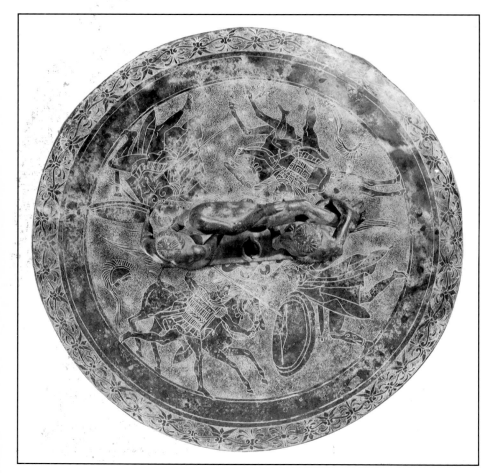

This detailed photograph of a cist from Praeneste now in Berlin presumably shows a Samnite infantryman attacking a dismounted cavalryman, possibly an Etruscan. The Samnite carries a scutum, a sword and a javelin, and wears a single greave on his left leg. This representation is highly important in providing archaeological evidence to support the contention of Livy and others that the Samnites fought with a single greave. (Photo: Berlin, Staatliche Museen)

in its chronology, is ultimately based on a relatively sound near-contemporary source. This information allows us to reconstruct a quite detailed picture of the Samnite army and perhaps, therefore, sheds some light on the versions of their tactics and equipment adopted by the Romans.

Livy tells us that in 310 the Samnite infantry all carried trapezoidal *scuta* which were wider at the top, in order to protect the breast and shoulders, with a level or flat top (i.e. not curving or oval in shape), but somewhat narrower at the bottom in order to allow better mobility. According to Livy the Samnite warriors wore a 'sponge' (*spongia*) in front of their breast. Clearly what is being described is the characteristic chest-protector (*pectorale*) widely worn during the fourth century, although it is a complete mystery why the word *spongia* is used. The left leg alone was covered with a greave. They wore crested helmets to make them appear taller. Spears are not mentioned, but if these Samnites were fighting in manipular formation the weapon used may have varied from maniple to maniple, some carrying a pair of javelins, others carrying spears.

Livy also tells us that the Samnite infantry was divided into two corps, each of which he calls an *exercitus* (usually translated as 'army'). The first wore tunics of bleached white linen and shields inlaid with silver. The other wore parti-coloured tunics and had shields inlaid with gold. An uncertain restoration in this section of Livy would also give baldrics and sheaths in silver to the first corps and in gold to the second. The first *exercitus* was given the post of honour on the right wing, while the second was drawn up on the left. Livy adds that it was the custom of the Samnites to consecrate themselves before battle, and this is why they dressed themselves in white and whitened their arms, for white was the colour of religious purity.

Further information is added by a second passage in Livy which describes the organization of the Samnite army before the Battle of Aquilonia in 293. A levy was held throughout Samnium, which, when concentrated at Aquilonia, amounted to 40,000 men. All who did not report for duty were to forfeit their life to Jupiter. In the middle of the camp an area some 60 metres (200 feet) in all directions was enclosed with wicker hurdles and was roofed over with linen. Here a sacrifice was made by Ovius Paccius according to ancient rites preserved on linen rolls in his possession. Livy mentions that the Samnite army

This terracotta statuette of Minerva shows the goddess carrying a trapezoidal shield. Such shields existed as gladiatorial weapons, but it would be unusual for the goddess to carry a purely gladiatorial weapon, rather than one also used in war. (Photo: Museo 'Sigismondo Castromediano', Lecce)

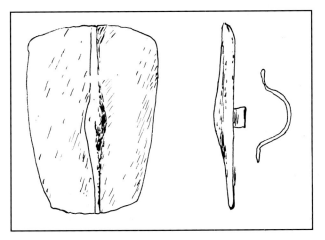

Gladiatorial relief from Venafro, dating from circa 50 BC, now walled in the entrance to the Palazzo Cimorelli. The right half of the lower register shows a fight between a 'Julian' Bassus and a 'Cassian' Chrestus. Bassus holds a 'trapezoidal' scutum. (Photo: Istituto Archeologico Germanico, Rome: Neg. Rom 31.3001; 75.2762)

was commanded by an *imperator*, perhaps Ovius Paccius himself. The *imperator* selected ten of the most eminent of the Samnites, and they then chose a further ten, until the number of the chosen band rose to 16,000 in strength. These soldiers then swore a solemn oath over the sacrifices, which were guarded by centurions with drawn swords. These were called the 'Linen Legion' (*legio linteata*) after the linen roof of the enclosure, and they were given splendid arms and crested helmets to distinguish them from the rest. The other *exercitus* comprised 'a little over twenty thousand men'; presumably 24,000 men to conform with the total of 40,000.

Livy gives the impression that the *legio linteata* had just been formed in the camp at Aquilonia in 293, but it is perfectly obvious that he is describing the same sacred band as was in operation in 310. On the eve of the Battle of Aquilonia Livy puts a speech in the mouth of Lucius Papirius, the Roman commander, who tells us that 'long ago' a silver and gilt Samnite army had been destroyed by his father. He seems to be referring to the conflict of 310 some 17 years previously. The whole speech, however, is best

regarded as a rhetorical embellishment by Livy. In the same passage he refers to the Samnite shields as being painted as well as silvered. This perhaps implies that the shields of the *legio linteata* were painted white, and only the metal components were decorated in silver. It seems obvious that Livy is manipulating the primary source which was available to him, and that the *legio linteata* was not a creation made just for the campaign of 293, but was rather a long-standing Samnite military institution. Assuming that the Romans were able to field a four-legion army of some 16,000 men or thereabouts regularly in the late fourth century, the Samnites may have felt compelled to create within their military system an élite force of comparable size, given better training than the rest of the army, to take the field against the Romans. Thus the *legio linteata* was a military institution comparable to the bodies of *epilektoi*, or 'picked' troops, formed by Greek armies, especially from the 360s onwards; a military institution which had already spread to the Syracusan army of Dionysius I in the early years of the century.

By adding some further details to the informa-

This famous pectorale, of the trilobate variety, was found in North Africa, where it had evidently been brought by an Italian mercenary in Carthaginian service. Colour photographs of the cuirass show it to be plated in white metal, either silver or tin, which suggests the possibility that it was an heirloom, and may even originally have been manufactured for use by a member of the legio linteata. A number of the decorative motifs, such as the bucranium fixing the shoulder plate, or the lintel decorated with paterae (flat bowls for sacrificial libations), supported by the columns of a temple colonnade, are concerned with sacrifice and perhaps refer to the sacrifice and oath taken by members of the legio linteata. The principal decorative feature is a head of Minerva wearing a triple-crested helmet, which follows Greek representations of Athena Promachos dating to the late fourth century. (Photo: Musée National de Bardo, Tunis)

tion imparted by Livy in these two passages, we can suggest a possible organizational structure for the *legio linteata*. The total citizen levy of the Samnite people which Livy mentions corresponds to the total citizen body (*touto*) of the Samnites, and the officer whom Livy calls an *imperator* may have been the chief civil and military magistrate of the Samnites, the *meddix tuticus*. Beneath him, the ten officers first selected may have been termed *meddices minores*, each in charge of a force of 1,600 *manipulares*, though we have no idea what these sub-units may have been called. Within his description of the events of 293 BC, Livy mentions 'the linen cohorts', and twenty cohorts of Samnites, each of about 400 men. Samnite cohorts of unspecified size are also mentioned in other passages. Elsewhere Livy mentions eight cohorts of Hernici operating in 362 BC, each numbering 400 men: that is, a total force of 3,200 men, double the size of one sub-unit of the *legio linteata*. Elsewhere in his *Histories* Livy uses terms such as maniple and cohort quite carelessly and anachronistically, but, given the combined weight of the passages mentioned above, it is difficult to avoid the conclusion that each of the ten divisions of the *legio linteata* numbering 1,600 men were divided into four cohorts of 400. Livy also mentions centurions in his description of the oath-taking, so it would be reasonable further to suggest that each of these cohorts was divided into two maniples and four centuries, each maniple having a *centurio prior* and *posterior* along the lines of later Roman practice.

The other *exercitus*, comprising the remainder of the Samnite infantry, would presumably have been divided along similar lines into 15 units of 1,600 men, each with its cohorts and maniples. If there were only two maniples to the cohort, it would be reasonable to deduce that the Samnite battle-line would have been drawn up into two lines of maniples, an *acies duplex*, with the first line of maniples equipped with javelins (*pila*), and the second line with fighting-spears (*hastae*).

The Manipular army in Livy

Livy (8.8) describes a Roman manipular formation drawn up in five lines. The first is composed of 15 maniples of *hastati* each with an extra 20 light-armed soldiers. The second line also has 15 maniples, this time of *principes*. Behind these stand in sequence the *triarii*, *rorarii*, and *accensi*. Livy gives few details concerning the equipment except that the light-armed *rorarii* and *accensi* have the javelin and spear, while the *triarii* have the *hasta*: all are armed with the *scutum*. We are left to assume that the *hastati* and *principes* were armed with the *pilum*. Nor is his description of tactical deployment complete. Livy speaks of the first three lines engaging the enemy one after the other, but he assigns no specific role to the *rorarii* and *accensi*. Although there is a certain internal logic in Livy's account, which makes a literal interpretation of his manipular system perfectly possible, severe doubts arise concerning the historicity of Livy's description. We know that *rorarii* was an early name for light-armed troops and that *accensi* were non-combatant baggage attendants (Varro). Neither of these pieces of information fits with Livy's description. A recent historian writing on this subject has said: 'This whole farrago appears as an antiquarian reconstruction, concocted out of scat-

Italo-Attic helmets of this type were in widespread use among the Samnites. This fourth century example, now in the British Museum, is said to have come from Vulci. (Photo: N.V. Sekunda)

tered pieces of information and misinformation, mostly to do with the manipular army. One of its underlying features seems to be a strained attempt to establish some sort of relation between the new military order and the five categories of the census classification.'

Livy's account must surely be rejected. We should rather assume that the Roman form of the manipular system had just three lines (of *hastati*, *principes* and *triarii*), plus attached light infantry (*rorarii*), from its very beginning. Elsewhere we have also assumed that it had roughly the same complement as the later Republican legion described by Polybius. It seems that Livy is basing his account on a source which describes how the *rorarii* retire behind the *triarii* following the initial phases of the battle,

The other type of pectorale most commonly in use among the Samnites and other Oscan peoples of south central Italy was the square variety, and it was this variety of pectoral which was later selected for use by the Roman army. This example, now in the British Museum, is south Italian and has been dated to c. 375–325 BC. Note the crude decoration in imitation of human musculature. (Photo: N.V. Sekunda).

and he is trying to integrate the *accensi*, who as baggage-carriers would stand behind the whole battle-line, into his account. As he is making the *accensi* combatants, Livy has to invent weapons for them to carry and consequently he has created an entirely spurious five-line formation with three rear lines.

Where we can suggest that the earlier form of the manipular legion differed from that of the second century BC is in the relative importance of the *pilum* and the *hasta*. In his account of the Battle of Beneventum (275 BC) Dionysius writes that 'those who fight in close combat with cavalry spears (i.e. hastae) held in the middle with both hands and who frequently achieve success in battle are called *principes* by the Romans'. Now we have good reason to believe that Dionysius' ultimate source at this point was a writer contemporary with the events of the Pyrrhic war, and it may even have been Pyrrhus' own court historian Proxenus. This makes the text unusually reliable and leads to the conclusion that in 275 the *principes* still used a thrusting spear (as the

triarii did even in the mid second century BC) and had not yet converted to the *pilum*. (E. Rawson, 'The Literary Sources for the Pre-Marian Army', *Papers of the British School at Rome* 39 (1971) 13–31.)

In the late fourth century BC, when manipular weapons and tactics were first introduced, it seems that the heavy javelin, later called a *pilum*, was called the *hasta velitaris*, and that the term *hasta* only came to be applied exclusively to the long fighting spear at a later date. Consequently, in the earliest Roman manipular formation, the only line which used the *hasta velitaris* was the first, and these were consequently given the name *hastati* – confusing to us who are more familiar with the later Republican army described by Polybius, in which only the last rank of *triarii* used the *hasta*. Thus in the earliest form of the manipular army only the first line comprising the *hastati* used the *pilum*. The *hastati*, as Dionysius implies, would have been used to break up the enemy formation before the *principes* moved in to secure a final victory with their long spears.

It has been suggested that this mosaic copies an original third century painting. It shows the sacrifice of a pig taking place inside a temple of Mars before a statue of the god. Three priests strike the carcass of the animal with sticks. The scene probably shows the solemnization of an oath of alliance, and the general idea seems to be that if the oath is broken, let the perpetrator be struck down by the god, 'As I strike this pig'. The scene has been compared with a passage in Livy where the carcass of a sacrificed pig is struck with flints rather than sticks. The scene also confirms that a connection existed between swine and the war-god. (Photo: Museo Borghese, Rome)

THE PLATES

A: The Earliest Roman Warriors, c. 700 BC

Had Romulus and Remus existed, they may have looked like these two figures.

A1 uses a helmet and shield based on those found in Esquiline Tomb 94. Tomb 94 also contained fragments of a chariot, including the iron tyres plus nails from the wheels, though these were insufficient to allow a restoration. Fragments of a wooden spear and iron spearhead were also found in Tomb 94, but were too decayed to enable recovery. Consequently the spear shown has been based on an example from Tomb 39 and the pectoral on one from Tomb 86. He carries a short sword of the 'Cuma' type found in Rome. We have no idea what personal dress may have looked like at this period in either Etruria or Latium, so these figures have been given rather coarse clothing decorated with a geometric pattern, as this was the dominating ornamental motif of the time. Whatever the precise form of dress, it would have been secured with bronze *fibulae*, which have

been recovered in quantity from a number of the warrior graves. Footwear of this period is a complete mystery. We have restored an ornamental boot of the Etruscan type, although representations of boots of this type with pointed toes are only present in Etruscan art *c*. 540–475 BC.

A2 uses military equipment entirely based on material from Esquiline findgroup 98, with the exception of the helmet, longsword and scabbard. The helmet is based on that once in the Zschille Collection; the sword an example of 'Rocca di Marro' type from Rome, and the scabbard on material found elsewhere. In the foreground lies an Etruscan warrior, based on military equipment found in tombs in Tarquinia. The huts in the background follow a model of the early Iron Age settlement on the Capitoline which was based on the excavated remains of the period.

B: Roman Warrior Bands, seventh century BC

B1 attempts to represent the appearance of a warrior in the seventh century, using the dress recorded for the Salii priests in the later Republican era. The decorated purple tunic known to have been worn by the Salii in the late Republican and Imperial periods may have been somewhat richer than that worn by their warrior predecessors. The cloak (*trabea*) is, in this case, not worn around the shoulders, but is rather worn 'in the Gabinian manner' (*cinctus Gabinus*), in other words rolled up and worn wound around the waist and/or shoulders. This style reputedly spread to Rome from the town of Gabii 12 miles east, which was allied to Rome after 493, though the ultimate origin may have been Etruscan. The cloak has been shown decorated with scarlet stripes and a purple border. The pectoral is based on that from Esquiline Tomb 14 although this is a little early for the seventh century.

B2 attempts to reconstruct the original dress of a *flamen* priest at this period. He wears the pointed

Detail from a red-figure crater in Leipzig dating to the first half of the fourth century, showing a Gallic horseman. Note the straight-bladed Celtic sword and the huge shield. The device painted onto the shield may be that of a particular war-band. The horseman is most probably naked behind the shield. His horse seems to be decorated with some form of body-paint and with bands of phalerae hung around its neck. (Photo: Antikenmuseum, Universität Leipzig)

helmet from which the *apex* supposedly derived, and the rounded cloak known as a *laena*, of Etruscan origin but ultimately derived from the Greek cloak known as a *chlaina*. The priest is dressed in white; the colour of ritual purity suitable for his office. In later Republican and Imperial times the *flamines* wore a distinctive boot. The practice of indicating rank by distinctive shapes and decorative elements in footwear seems to have been Etruscan in origin and to have spread to Rome. The *flamen* is shown wearing white boots of a distinctive shape drawn from an Etruscan statuette.

C: Horatius at the Bridge, 508 BC

Around 509 BC the last Etruscan king, Tarquinius Superbus, was expelled from Rome and appealed to the king of Clusium, Lars Porsenna, who may also have been head of the Etruscan League at this time, to restore him to the Roman throne. Porsenna marched on Rome and seized the Janiculum in a sudden attack; the way lay open to the rest of the city across the Tiber. Livy records a story that Horatius Cocles rushed to the bridge, together with Spurius Larcius and Titus Herminius, and together the three held back the whole Etruscan army, while behind them work continued feverishly on the demolition of the bridge. When scarcely anything was left of the bridge Horatius sent back the two others and carried on the fight alone. With a crash and a deafening shout from the Romans the bridge finally fell. Horatius invoked Father Tiber, leaped into the river, and swam to the bank and safety.

The three figures are based on polychrome representations of hoplites dating to the late sixth or early fifth centuries BC.

C1 is based on a fragment from the central acroterium of the Sassi Caduti temple at Falerii Veteres, and so represents an Etruscan hoplite of the period.

C2 is based on the painted terracotta body of an Amazon from the pediment of a temple on the Esquiline hill. It is highly debatable whether this decorated fragment can be taken as an accurate reflection of the dress of a Roman warrior of the early fifth century. The style and decoration of the cuirass is of a type normally found specifically on representations of Amazons, and is not really appropriate for a male Roman warrior. Furthermore the sculpture is of

This Roman gold stater, dating to 218 BC, shows on its reverse Italian and Roman generals swearing an oath of alliance over a pig (J.P.C. Kent and Max and Albert Hirmer, Roman Coins (1978) no. 14, pl. 7). Note the muscle–cuirass worn by the Roman general, and the decorative point to his lance, which may be a badge of his rank. (Photo: Hirmer Fotoarchiv, München)

Greek workmanship, and the representational style is clearly Greek. Nevertheless we have incorporated the sculpture within this plate, in order to use all sources of representational evidence in colour for the period.

C3 is based on a fragment of a fictile plaque from the temple of Mater Matuta in Satricum. Latin hoplites are not known to have fought as allies of Lars Porsenna, but he is known to have used mercenary troops. One piece of evidence for this is the story of Mucius Scaevola who attempted to assassinate the Etruscan king in his camp, but by mistake killed the king's scribe, who was paying out money to the army.

D: The Venetic Fighting System, fifth century BC

This plate is based on the figures from the Certosa Situla, representing the various components of the Venetic battle-line. As it would not be practicable to depict full scale maniples in any detail, we have shown the troop types as four single advancing lines.

The reconstruction of the shield of **D1** has not

been straightforward, as it is impossible to tell whether the main body of the shield shown is intended to be non-metallic, with only the rim and boss in bronze, or whether the whole shield is supposed to be covered in a bronze facing. Similarly with *D2* it is not clear whether the shields are non-metallic or covered in bronze sheeting. Here we have followed Peter Connolly in showing the shields as non-metallic but with bronze bosses.

D3 has been shown with bronze hoplite shields. In the sixth century the Greek hoplite shield had a bronze rim, a bronze internal vertical handle for the elbow, and sometimes a bronze shield device attached to the front. The rest of the shield consisted of multiple layers of ox-hide. At the turn of the century,

at a date which cannot be specified precisely, the entire shield becomes faced with a thin bronze sheet, stressed to give it strength. Thus we cannot be sure whether we should show these Venetic warriors with bronze-faced shields or not. These Venetic shields seem to be of local manufacture – the triangular decoration of the shield-rim is in stark contrast to the multiple cable pattern found on the overwhelming majority of hoplite shields manufactured on the Greek mainland. We have also given these hoplites bronze greaves, although these are not shown on the situla.

D4 represents the group of Venetic axemen shown on the Certosa Situla. The precise details of the cuirass cannot be worked out from the situla, and we have interpreted the cuirass as being of different coloured heavy linen or other textile material, not unlike the Greek *spolas*. The situla as a whole conveys the impression that there was some standardization of dress and equipment, but this is surely just an artistic device. It is difficult to believe that there was anything approaching state issue of equipment and uniformity of dress among the Veneti at a date as early as this.

E: Roman Hoplites defeated by Celts, fourth century BC

During the fourth century central Italy, including Latium, was subjected to periodic invasions by Gallic tribes. This plate depicts the rout of a Roman army during one of these battles.

E1 is based on the fourth century ivory plaques from Praeneste, *E2* is based on the François Tomb and *E3* is based on the cist in St Petersburg. The uniformity

Fragment of a tomb-painting from the Esquiline possibly copying one of the series of historical frescoes painted by Fabius Pictor to decorate the Temple of Salus in 304. The Samnite general (left) is labelled as Marcus Fannius, the Roman as Q. Fabius; perhaps Q. Fabius Maximus Rullianus, dictator in 315. The scene may, therefore, represent the surrender of a Samnite city during this year. The Samnite wears a Montefortino helmet with 'wing' plumes at the side (pennae), a goat-skin cloak, a white subligaculum (lion-cloth) and two greaves, and carries a huge oval shield. The Roman general is shown carrying a long fighting hasta as a badge of his office, and is draped in his cloak (paludamentum). Behind him his cohors praetoria is drawn up, carrying long hastae and dressed in white tunics, as was the practice in later Roman armies.

Two details taken from a Praenestine situla in Berlin. The situla as a whole shows a scene of sacrifice, attended by a Roman general carrying an eagle-standard, and a member of his entourage carrying a lituus; a badge of office of Etruscan origin. The lituus-bearer wears boots with ornamental folded-down tops, perhaps precursors of those worn by members of the equestrian order, and a pair of greaves. (Photo: Berlin, Staatliche Museen)

of the muscle-cuirasses and greaves is remarkable, and can perhaps be taken as evidence for at least some kind of standardization of military equipment within the Roman hoplite army in the fourth century. The red colour of the tunics is taken from the François Tomb painting. The shield device of *E2*, the head of a minotaur, is based on an Etruscan mirror, but the 'legionary' shield blazons of the other figures are loosely based on Republican coinage. The fourth century archaeological sources on which these figures are based invariably show Latin hoplites clean-shaven, which is something of a paradox, as tradition maintained that the first barbers only came to Rome in the third century BC.

E4 is based on a red-figure crater in Leipzig, while *E5* is based on a third century wall painting from the Esquiline, now in the Palazzo dei Conservatori, Rome.

F: Samnite Warriors, c. 293 BC
This plate attempts a reconstruction of the dress which might have been worn by the Samnite army at the Battle of Aquilonia in 293.

F1 attempts to reconstruct the appearance of a soldier of the *legio linteata*. All his weapons and dress are either whitened or silvered. The cuirass is based on the Bardo cuirass, while the helmet (note the crest, mentioned by Livy) and the greave repeat the same decorative motifs found on the cuirass.

F2, together with various figures in the background, represents the balance of the Samnite army, dressed in their 'parti-coloured' tunics. The Samnite tunic was extremely short and curved at the bottom, so as to cover the genitalia, and had short sleeves, like a modern T-shirt. Bands of decorated material were applied at the shoulder, sleeves, hem, chest, etc., as in these examples, which are based on paintings of warriors from Paestan tombs and Lucanian vases. The decorative colours and motifs have been repeated on the shields. Whether their arms were truly gilded, or whether this is a hyperbole (for bronze weapons) of Livy or of his source, is not known. Some warriors carry spears, and some carry javelins based on the Vulci javelin.

G: Sacrifice establishing a treaty between Romans and Samnites
The central and background scene in this plate is based on the mosaic in the Museo Borghese depicting a sacrifice held before Mars.

G1 and *G2* are based on two figures from a Praenestine situla in Berlin. Both wear olive wreaths,

This oval shield, shown on a Roman aes signatum coin of five Roman pounds which was struck about 280 BC, is presumably of the type carried by the Roman legionary of the period. There remains the possibility, however, that it may be shown as an item of booty.

A second example of Roman bronze bar coinage, also struck in the early third century, shows a sword and a scabbard with baldric, both of distinctively Greek type. Again the equipment shown is presumably Roman, and if so this coin confirms that the Spanish sword had not yet been adopted by the Roman army.

probably symbols of victory in this context, which may be taken as an indication that the general is a *triumphator* celebrating his triumph, which would, in turn, explain his extremely complex dress. The literary sources are somewhat confused as to whether and under what circumstances Roman generals wore crimson or scarlet, which has made the reconstruction of the colours for these two figures somewhat problematical. We have in the end decided on scarlet with heavy gold embroidery. The general wears a cloak with a border measuring a palm's width, heavily embroidered in gold.

G2 is based on the figure of the Samnite general Marcus Fannius from a historical painting found in a tomb on the Esquiline.

H: Roman Hastati *fight one of Pyrrhus'* *elephants*

The Epirote war elephant is based on a contemporary representation of an elephant and its calf on a painted plate now in the Museo Nazionale di Villa Giulia. It is clear from the painting that the crew wear muscle-cuirasses (the naveal is quite clear on the driver's cuirass). Their tunics, as well as the housing of the elephant, are dark crimson. The helmets have a triple plume, most probably of white horsehair. The yellow-painted tower on the elephant's back (presumably wooden) is protected on each side by a bronze hoplite shield, and is held in place by three thick chains.

The elephant is shown in conflict with a maniple of Roman *hastati*. The *hastati* are shown without muscle-cuirass, coat of mail, or *pectorale*. The tendency seems to have been for the *manipularii* of all three ranks to have become progressively more heavily equipped as time passed; thus in the late Republic all *manipularii* wore coats of mail. The Roman troops wear Montefortino helmets, and carry swords and shields based on *aes grave* coins. They have been supplied with a single greave on the leading leg, which has been based on those worn by the *lituus*-bearer shown on a Praenestine situla.

The legionaries of the Roman Imperial army are known to have worn tunics of a natural off-white colour. This 'uniformly' drab appearance may well have come about in the Roman army following its massive expansion in the middle of the fourth century, the mass of new Roman warriors repeatedly pressed into service choosing to clothe themselves in the cheapest undyed cloth. For similar reasons of cost the rapidly expanding armies of the Bourbon and Hapsburg monarchies adopted uniform clothing in cheap natural colours at the end of the 17th century of our era.

Locri had at first supported Pyrrhus, but, when Rome confirmed her independence after the defeat of Pyrrhus, she declared her loyalty to Rome on this coin, struck c. 274. Pistis 'loyalty' is here shown crowning Roma. Note the oval shield, with rim, spine and boss, used by Roma. This archaeological evidence confirms that the scutum was used by the Roman army by this date, and also gives us its precise size and appearance. (Photo: N.V. Sekunda)

REPUBLICAN ROMAN ARMY 200-104 BC

INTRODUCTION

Researchers have directed most of their effort towards the Roman Army during the Imperial period. This is hardly surprising. The Roman Imperial Army is a unique phenomenon. It is difficult to think of any other state in any historical period which managed to maintain such a large, entirely professional army for such a long time. This fact alone dictates that the Imperial Army will continue to receive the attention it deserves.

Consequently the Imperial Army is well understood, but the same cannot be said of the Republican. The further one goes back in time, the less is known about the Roman Army. The military reforms carried out by Marius between 107 and 104 BC constitute a watershed in our knowledge. After this date we have sufficient literary and archaeological evidence to give us a reasonable outline (see Harmand). The legionary organisation which Marius' reforms crystallized is attested in numerous literary passages, while the archaeological monuments, beginning with the 'Altar of Domitius Ahenobarbus', probably recording the census of Cn. Domitius Ahenobarbus in 115 BC (Torelli 5-16), show us Republican legionaries at the end of the 2nd century almost universally equipped in mail.

Before this date the situation is far from clear. Elizabeth Rawson, a pre-eminent scholar of the Roman Republic, summarised the situation thus (13): 'The subject of the arms and organisation of the Roman army in and before the mid-second century BC is one of almost inextricable confusion.' Little has changed in the two decades or more since these words were written.

Few historians have dealt with the earlier army at all, and the only lengthy treatment of the subject is that of Eduard Meyer. Brief accounts of the pre-Marian army are also given by Parker (9-20) and Keppie (14-56), and a more extended treatment by Peter Conolly (86-207). No military

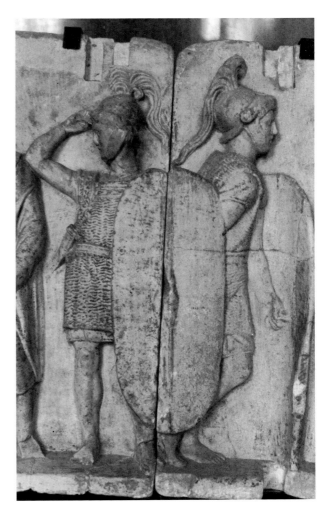

Legionaries from the **Altar of Domitius Ahenobarbus.** *(Photo: author)*

archaeologist can fail, at this point, to mention the remarkable excavations made by Adolf Schulten of the Roman camps in the region of Numantia in the period 1903-12. A book of this size cannot throw light on all aspects of the Roman Republican Army, but it can at least provide an outline of the equipment and organization of the army in the 2nd century, a time when Rome was growing from a regional to a world power.

INFANTRY EQUIPMENT

The principal source of information on both the equipment and the organization of the Roman Republican Army is the sixth book of the *Histories* of the Greek historian Polybius, written a little before 150 BC (Walbank, *Commentary* I, 636). Polybius was born about 200 BC, served as *hipparchos* of the Achaean League in 170/69, and wrote a book *On Tactics*. After Pydna, Polybius was among the 1,000 prominent Achaeans who were deported to Rome. There he became friends with Scipio Aemilianus, and accompanied him on his various travels, witnessing, among other things, the destruction of Carthage in 146. Polybius was, then, uniquely qualified to write on the subject of the Roman Army, and his description of Roman military equipment is probably based on his own experience and observation.

The Roman shield

Polybius (6. 23. 2-5) gives a complete account of the Roman shield. It had a curved surface approximately 75 cm wide and 1.4 m high, and a span of 10 cm. (Here Polybius probably means that the rim curved back a span from the front of the shield.)(Treloar). It was made of 'double planking'; presumably two layers of wooden ply glued together and then covered on the outer side first with canvas and then with leather. The rim had an iron trim on its upper and lower edges, protecting the shield against sword-blows from above and against the earth below. It also had an iron boss which would have turned aside the heaviest blows from missiles.

The ancient authorities inform us that the Roman shield was of Samnite (Athen. 6. 273 f) or Sabine (Plut. *Vit. Rom.* 21. 1) origin (cf. Eichberg 171-5). Perhaps large wooden shields of this type were ultimately of Celtic origin.

The Kasr el-Harit shield was found in the Egyptian Fayum by an English team of papyrologists in 1900. Its measurements correspond remarkably well to the dimensions given by Polybius. However, the shield has no iron rim or boss, and is oval rather than round in shape. It is covered in woollen felt on both sides, the inner lining overlapping the outer by 50-60 mm. The body of the shield is made up of three layers of thin wooden segments running in alternate directions, vertically and horizontally. The segments on the outside and inside of the shield, between 25 and 50 mm wide, run horizontally; the inner side of the shield comprising 40 segments. The middle layer comprises ten segments, 60-100 mm wide, running vertically.

For the method of construction we may compare Varro (Ling. 5. 115), who tells us that the Latin word *scutum* is derived from *sectura* or 'cutting', because it is made of wood cut into small pieces. Whatever the truth of Varro's etymology,

Senior officer, possibly a tribune, from the **Altar of Domitius Ahenobarbus.** *(photo: author)*

Right *Cavalryman from the* **Altar of Domitius Ahenobarbus.** *(photo: author)*

he confirms that the Roman shield was made from ply. Kimmig thought the Kasr el-Harit shield was probably made of birch wood. Pliny (*NH* 16. 209) tells us that the most suitable woods for making shields are those in which an incision causes the wood to draw together at once and close its own wound; these include vine, willow, lime, birch, elder and both kinds of poplar.

At the centre of the shield is a wooden 'barley-corn' boss, attached with iron nails, with a wooden *spina* running above and below to the rim. The remains of iron rings for attaching carrying-straps are also found on the inside of the shield. Peter Connolly produced a reconstruction of the Kasr el-Harit shield which weighed 10 kg. The shield was found among houses which all seemed to belong to the late Ptolemaic period, which led Kimmig, the original publisher, to suggest that the shield had belonged to a Celtic mercenary in Ptolemaic service. Later commentators have suggested that the shield is Roman. As the late Ptolemaic army adopted Roman military equipment, certainty in this matter is impossible.

Vegetius (2. 18) informs us that each cohort painted different signs on their shields, and each

Above *This sculpture, from the Basilica Aemilia in the Roman Forum, shows the legend of Tarpeia, who offered to betray Rome to the Sabines in return for 'what they wore on their left arms'; meaning their gold ornaments. As they passed Tarpeia they killed her by throwing their shields upon her. The Basilica was first erected in 179, but was reconstructed many times subsequently, which makes dating any individual sculpture most uncertain. Some authorities (Bandinelli & Torelli fig. 49) would attribute this particular sculpture to the Sullan reconstruction phase of 87-78. The shield is decorated with a winged animal, possibly a feline, but more probably a horse. The 'Pegasus' is a common coin blazon of many Italian cities of the Republican period. Its significance is unknown but the sculptor evidently thought it a suitable device for a Sabine. (Photo: Deutschen Archäologischen Instituts, Rome)*

soldier wrote his name, his cohort and his century on the back. This may have been the practice in the Imperial period, but we have no unequivocal evidence that the different units of the Roman Army decorated their shields in any distinctive way in the Republican period. Livy (27. 47. 1) describes how in 207 BC, on the eve of the Battle of the Metaurus River, Hasdrubal observed among the enemy old shields which he had not seen before. The Roman Army had been reinforced by the Second Consular Army following a forced march. It seems that Hasdrubal can distinguish the 'new' old shields from the normal shields he was familiar with, and the natural way in which to

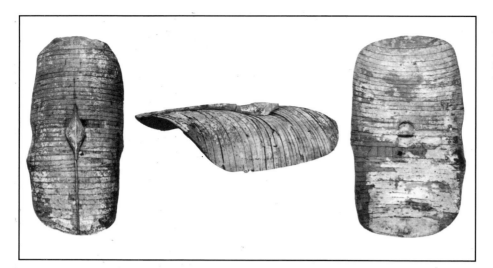

Photograph of the Kasr el-Harit shield, (left) outside (centre) side and (right) inside, taken from the original publication. (Photo after Kimmig)

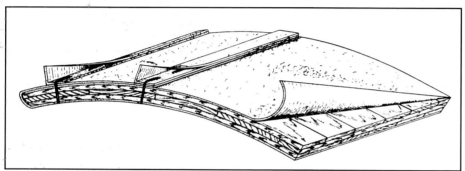

Cross-section showing the triple-ply construction. Polybius probably examined a number of Roman shields, but only visually. This could be the reason why he states that the shield is constructed from 'double planking', rather than triple. (Drawing after Kimmig 108 fig. 1)

interpret this passage would be to assume that the 'new' old shields had different shield devices which Hasdrubal had not seen before. This is hardly, however, a passage on which to pin any conclusive argument.

Frontinus (*Strat.*, 4. 1. 5) records that Scipio Africanus, upon taking over command of the Roman Army besieging Numantia in 134 BC, saw a soldier with an elegantly decorated shield. Scipio remarked that he didn't wonder that the soldier had decorated it with such care, since he obviously put more trust in it than in his sword. It is not immediately obvious whether this passage implies that each soldier decorated his own shield as he wished, or simply that the individual soldier was responsible for decorating his own shield in the pattern prescribed for his unit. Furthermore, the anecdote may not be genuinely recorded, for other versions of the story (eg. Livy, *Per.* 57) make the size of the shield the point of the story, not its decoration. Finally, Silius Italicus (17. 395-

8) gives Scipio a shield decorated with effigies of his father and uncle in battle

Helmets

During the 2nd century soldiers of the Roman Army were obliged to supply their own equipment, or at least their arms were their own property. Consequently, we should not expect to find complete uniformity in dress or equipment. As the 2nd century progressed the demand for military equipment increased as a result of incessant war and an ever-increasing scale of mobilisation. At the end of the 2nd century Marius was recruiting volunteers from the lowest property classes into the legions, and these troops would have been unable to bring their own arms with them.

Most helmets surviving from the Republican period are of the 'Montefortino' type, named after the cemetery of Montefortino in Ancona, from which a large number were excavated. A number come from battle-sites in Greece (Calligas). Until the end of the 2nd century the bowls of the helmet were decorated and finished well, with the brim ending in a fine rope-work coil. Some 2nd-century helmets are stamped with an armourer's mark countersunk into the bronze with a die, implying some form of mass-production even at this early date. There was, however, a marked deterioration towards the end of the century, as demand increased. Even so, helmets continued to be produced by hammering; spinning only seems to have come in during the early years of the Principate (Paddock).

The earlier examples of the Montefortino helmet come together into something of a point at the top. Varro (*Ling.* 5. 115) tells us that the type of helmet known as *conus* is so-called because it narrows (*cogitur*) towards the top. Thus the term *conus* may have been a specific word for the Montefortino type. The Greeks also used the word *konos* of a certain type of helmet; obviously a borrowing has taken place, though it is not clear which way round.

At the top of the bowl of the helmet was a crest-knob, filled with lead and then drilled with a hole in the middle for the insertion of a crest-pin. Thus the crest-pin was held firmly in an upright position (Russell Robinson 14). The crest consisted of what Polybius (6. 23. 12) calls a feathered 'wreath' or 'crown', with three straight crimson or black feathers stretching above, about a cubit (45 cm) in length. The latter must have been wing-feathers taken from some very large bird. Statius, a poet of the Flavian period, describes some mythical Spartans wearing 'Ledaean' crests (i.e. of swans' feathers). Virgil (*Aen.* 10. 185-193) also has the Ligurian heroes Cunerus and Cupavo wear crests of swans' feathers. (The swans of the river Po were famous in antiquity.) The nature of the wreath or crown beneath the crest proper is not known. It may have resembled the white band (*infula*) wound into the scarlet crest of another helmet (*conus*) described by Statius (*Theb.* 4. 218).

The Montefortino helmet has become the standard helmet worn by all modern reconstructions of the Roman soldier during the 2nd century BC. However, it may not have been the only type of helmet in use. The Italo-Corinthian and the Italo-Attic types had earlier been very popular too,

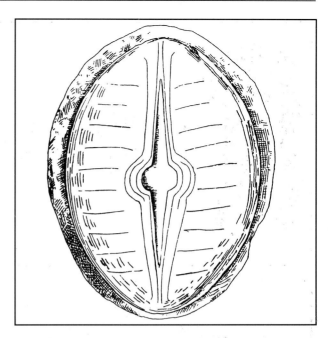

The ply construction of the shield is demonstrated by this funerary sculpture from Vetulonia, normally dated to the early seventh century. (After Studi Etruschi 21 (1950-51) p. 28 fig. 3)

especially in regions to the south of Rome, such as Campania or Apulia. These may have continued in use into the 2nd century, though examples have not survived – perhaps due to the end of rich burials in this region. The Italo-Attic type had been especially popular among the Samnites, and did continue in use: it developed into the Imperial-Italic type, which emerged in the 1st century AD (Russell Robinson 62).

The cuirass

Polybius (6. 23. 14) informs us that those who were rated in the census-class above 10,000 drachmas wore a coat of mail armour (*lorica hamata*), which was of Gallic origin (Varro, *Ling.* 5. 116). A leather jerkin called the *thoracomachus* was probably worn under the mail shirt in this period, as in later periods (*De Rebus Bellicis* 15). A law passed during the first tribunate of C. Gracchus in 123 BC provided for the free distribution of arms to every single citizen-soldier in the army, at public expense (Gabba 6-7), and it seems reasonable to assume that all legionaries would be issued with mail cuirasses after that date.

Polybius, writing decades before the free distribution of arms was introduced, tells us (6. 23. 14) that the majority of the heavy infantry wore the *kardiophylax*, or 'heart-protector' (*pectorale*), a bronze sheet about 22.5 cm square placed in front of the chest and kept in place by leather thongs (Varro, *Ling.* 5. 116). Polybius is not, therefore, describing the 'Campanian' *pectorale* of triple disc shape, or the round *pectorale* worn by the mountain tribes of the central highlands, such as the Hernici, Aequi and Volsci (Connolly 101). Rather the shape had developed out of the square breastplates worn by the Samnites (Connolly 110-111) and adopted after early military contacts with them. In fact Pliny (*HN* 34. 43) does mention that following his defeat of the Samnites in 293, Spurius Carvilius made a statue of Jupiter Capitolinus from their captured 'heart-protectors', greaves and helmets. No contemporary square *pectorale* has survived. It has been suggested that a round bronze disc, 170 mm in diameter, recovered from Numantia, might be a *pectorale* (Bishop & Coulston 59). The pectorale may have disappeared from use soon after Polybius description, replaced by the mail shirt.

A third type of cuirass, the muscle-cuirass, must also be considered. Though not mentioned by Polybius, a large number of examples have been recovered from graves in Campania and elsewhere, and representations continue to show the muscle-cuirass in use into the 1st century BC. Of the infantrymen shown fighting on the Roman side on the Aemilius Paulus monument, two wear mail shirts, but three wear muscle-cuirasses (Kähler).

Greaves

Polybius (6. 23. 8) only mentions 'greave' in the singular, indicating that only one greave was worn. The wearing of the single greave may have been a native Italian practice. Livy (9. 40. 3) mentions that the Samnites wore a single greave on their left leg during a battle with the Romans in 310 BC. Following the Samnite defeat, the Campanians equipped their gladiators in this way, and called them Samnites (9. 40. 17). In Rome Decimus Junius Brutus was the first Roman to give a gladiatorial exhibition in memory of his dead father, in 264 BC (Livy, *Per.* xvi). Subsequently a single greave on the left leg was regularly worn by that class of gladiator called 'Samnite' (Juvenal 6. 256-7; cf. Silus Italicus, *Punica* 8. 419; Virgil, *Aen.* 7. 685-690). Representations of the late Republican period showing armed men wearing a single greave on the left leg generally represent gladiators, and no unequivocal representations of soldiers wearing a

The mail cuirass was also ultimately of Celtic origin. This statuette of a Gaul, from Baratela, Este, shows a cuirass not fitted with shoulder-guards after the Greek fashion. Rather, in the Celtic fashion, the mail falls over the shoulders in two flaps, secured by a clasp in front of the chest. (Drawing after Montelius)

single greave have survived. The Aemilius Paulus monument and later representations of Roman legionaries do not show any greaves being worn, so the single greave was possibly abandoned early in the 2nd century.

The pilum

Polybius (6. 23. 9-11) tells us that *pila* were constructed thus: a barbed iron head 1.35 m long was inserted for about half its length into a wooden haft of the same length and was riveted securely in place. The total length of the *pilum* was 1.8 m. Where it met the wooden haft the iron head was about 3.75 cm thick. Examples of such *pila* have been recovered from the Roman camps around Numantia (Bishop & Coulston 50), upon which source Peter Connolly (131) has based his reconstructions. The iron head of the javelin, designed for use against more distant targets, was attached to the haft by a socket.

The *pilum* was primarily thrown with the aim of killing the enemy, but if it didn't kill, it was designed to render the shields of the enemy unusable. A single *pilum* might pierce two separate shields and fix them together, or the iron of the extended socket might become so bent that it couldn't be plucked out of the shield (Caes., *Bell.*

Infantrymen from the Aemilius Paulus Monument. The Roman forces raised for the Third Macedonian War included 2,000 Ligurians (Livy 42. 35. 5-6). The two figures on the right, *from a part of the frieze showing the start of the battle, wear muscle-cuirasses with large rolled-over rims at the bottom and could represent the Ligurian infantry who were involved in the opening skirmish. The very large, almost hexagonal, shields could be the Ligurian shields specifically mentioned by Livy 44. 35.19. Note the drill-holes at the waist for the attachment of model swords in bronze. (Photos after Kähler, pls. 14, 6)*

Gall. 1. 25. 3). Plutarch (*Vit.Mar.* 25. 1-2) describes the famous improvisation which Marius made to the *pilum* shortly before the Battle of Vercellae, against the Cimbri in 101 BC. Up to this time, Plutarch says, the iron head was fastened to the shaft with two iron rivets. Marius replaced one of these with a wooden peg. When the *pilum* struck the enemy's shield, the wooden peg sheared while the single iron peg stayed intact. The iron head stuck fast in the shield, while the wooden haft jack-knifed, swung downwards and dangled from the single iron peg, trailing along the ground at an angle.

The Spanish sword (*gladius*)

All heavy infantry carried a Spanish sword at the right hip. It was an excellent thrusting weapon, since the blade was very strong and firm, and

Left and right This terra-cotta from Caere, probably the war god (Maule & Smith 5), may represent the appearance of an allied infantryman in the 2nd century. He is saluting with his right hand. Note the muscle-cuirass, sword hilt and shield, and helmet with raised cheek-pieces. (Photo & drawing: Staatliche Museen zu Berlin Preussischer Kulturbesitz Antiken - Sammlung)

This bronze figure, once in the Collection Gréau, shows a bearded male, possibly a soldier rather than a gladiator, wearing a cloak, the short Samnite tunic with wide belt, and a single greave on the left leg. (Drawing after Froehner, no. 1037)

both its edges cut effectively (Polyb. 6. 23. 6-7). The Spanish sword made a tremendous impact on the Macedonians. Livy (31. 34. 4) describes the dismay which swept through the Macedonian army when they saw what damage the Spanish sword had inflicted on the bodies of the dead during a skirmish in the early stages of the Second Macedonian War. In many it had severed limbs or decapitated the corpses. According to Polybius, the Spanish sword was adopted during the Second Punic War, but its adoption may have taken place earlier (Walbank, I 704, III 754).

A fragment from Poseidonius (Diodorus 5. 33.

3-4), who had travelled extensively in the western Mediterranean, describes the weapons of the Celtiberians. They carried swords which were two-edged and wrought of excellent iron, and had daggers 22.5 cm long which they used when fighting at close quarters. He describes how they used to bury iron plates in the ground and wait till the rust had eaten away all the softest metal. They then worked the remaining, most unyielding, steel into excellent swords. The Roman military dagger (*pugio*), presumably also of Spanish origin, is not mentioned by Polybius, and may have only been adopted by the Romans in the later 2nd or even the 1st century (Bishop & Coulston 54-5).

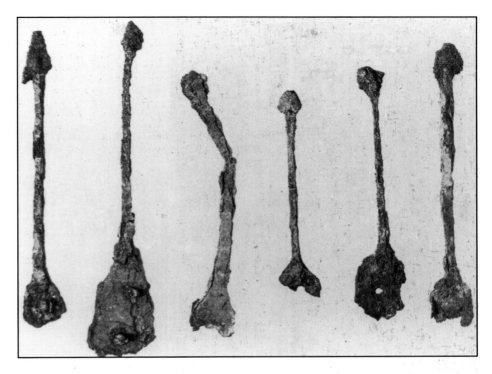

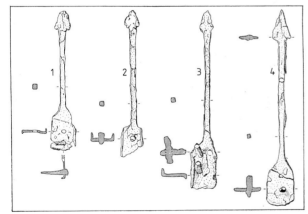

ORGANIZATION OF THE LEGIONS

Polybius' description of the administration of the military oath, or of the setting-out of the camp, are described from the point of view of the military tribunes. Consequently Rawson (15) has suggested that one of his literary sources consisted of some *commentarii* of military tribunes. These probably took the form of records of, or directions for, a single event. Cato the Elder (234-149 BC)

wrote a work entitled *De Re Militari*. The surviving fragments take the form of a handbook of practical information concerning Roman military practices (Astin 184), similar in style to the *commentarii* used by Polybius. The date of its composition is unknown, though it is probable that all of Cato's written works were composed in his later years, thus at about the same time Polybius was writing book six. When Polybius comes to the levying of the cavalry he does so after dealing with the levying of the infantry, and he corrects himself to say that in reality the cavalry is now levied first, making it clear that his source is not absolutely contemporary. It is unlikely, however, that his account is very far out of date (Rawson 14–15).

The levy

Service in the legions was the right and the duty of the *adsidui*, the body of the citizenry owning property of at least 400 denarii in value and so able to support themselves financially (Keppie 33). A census was held every five years, in which the *adsidui* were registered in tribes and distributed into five classes according to wealth. The census concluded with a religious ceremony of purification, known as the 'lustration' (*lustratio*). The *pro-*

letarii, citizens whose property fell below the minimum levy for inclusion in the census classes, were not normally required to serve in the legions during this period, other than in times of dire emergency. Roman males became eligible for military service during their 17th year (Gell., *NA* 10. 28), and were only required to perform military service, as *iuniores*, until their 46th (Cic., *de sen.* 60). In times of emergency, such as the mobilisation of 171 BC for the Third Macedonian War, the oath could be administered to the *seniores* up to their 50th year (Livy 40. 26. 7; see Taylor 86). Normally citizens were required to perform six years of service continuously in the same legion, or sometimes in separate levies. They could serve as long as 16 years in the infantry or ten in the cavalry, and even longer as a volunteer. When an army was levied, the citizens would meet in a *dilectus*, or 'choosing', at which they were allocated to the various legions. Infantry were paid one third of a *denarius* daily, cavalry a full *denarius*, and from this deductions were made for food and equipment (Keppie 33-4).

The legion

The basic unit of the Roman Army was the legion. *Legere* means 'to gather together' and the word 'legion' means a force gathered together in the levy (Varro, *Ling.* 5. 87; cf. Plut., *Vit. Rom.* 13. 1). Under normal circumstances the army

A Roman military road near Antioch in northern Syria. The Roman military historian Boris Rankov is walking along it to demon- *strate that it was designed to be capable of accommodating a legionary* **contuburnium** *marching six abreast. (Photo: author)*

numbered four urban legions (*legiones urbanae* Polyb. 6. 19. 7), two under the command of each of the two consuls. The consular legions would normally be numbered I to IV. During the Second Punic War there were upwards of 20 legions in the field, and it may well have been during this period that the supplementary legions started to be numbered on a regular basis.

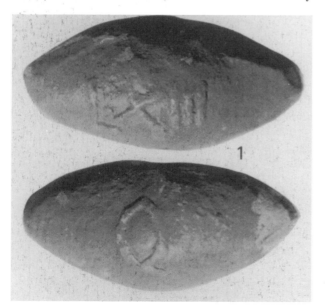

Moulded slingbullets bearing the inscription L. XIII, standing for legio XIII, have been found in Spain, deposited by the Scipionic forces attacking the Carthaginian camp at Gandul during the final phases of the Second Punic War. They can probably be associated with the 13th *Legion which Livy (29. 2. 9) informs us was serving there in 205. On their reverse the bullets have the letter Q, and other bullets have the letter A in Etruscan cursive script, indicating the area of recruitment of their users. (Photos: L. Villaronga)*

Numbered legions are also mentioned participating in the Istrian expedition of the consul A. Manlius Vulso in 178 BC (Agnew).

Each legion had six tribunes attached to it (Polyb. 6. 19. 8-9). Service as a tribune brought great honour, and even ex-consuls would serve as tribunes (Suolahti; Keppie 39). Normally the six tribunes divided themselves into three pairs, each pair taking it in turns to command the legion for two months (Polyb. 6. 34. 3). (The pair may have taken it in turns to command the legion on alternate days (Walbank II 583-4).) In the Imperial period the legion was commanded by a *legatus*. Polybius does not refer to military *legati*: they became increasingly common as the 2nd century drew on, though still not as legionary commanders (Rawson 19; cf. Keppie 40).

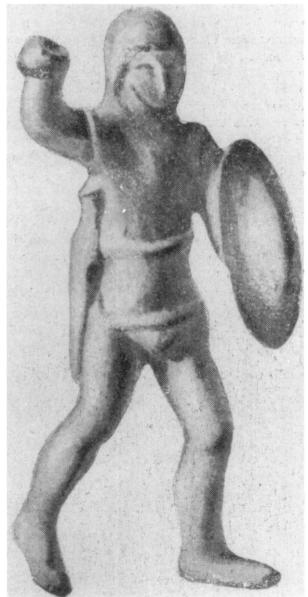

Third-century bronze statuette, height 7 cm, in the Villa Giulia, Rome, possibly representing a veles. *Note the covering to the head, the* parma velitaris, *and the sword by his side. (Drawing after Ausonia 2 (1907) 281 fig. 2; photo Sopr. Arch. Etruria Meridionale)*

The cohort

The legion had a strength of 4,200 infantry (Polyb. 6. 20. 8). Later on it was divided into ten cohorts, each numbering 420. Polybius describes the way in which the officers of the legion were selected. This need not imply that the cohort didn't exist as a tactical sub-division of the legion, for Polybius, reflecting the interests of his source, doesn't explicitly describe the organization of the legion: rather he is concerned with the duties of the tribunes, such as the way in which the military oath is administered

Livy (22. 38. 2) tells us that the military oath was first administered to the army by the tribunes in 216 BC, on the eve of the Battle of Cannae. Previously there had only been a general oath to assemble upon the orders of the consuls, and an oath taken by the centuries of infantry and decuries of cavalry not to leave the ranks. Rawson (17) has noted that if Livy is correct upon this matter, a *terminus ante quem* of 216 BC is supplied for the literary sources of Polybius. In all likelihood his sources will, in fact, be considerably later than that date.

Some gladiators on foot used the **parma velitaris** *too. This comic figurine in the Louvre, from Smyrna, shows an ape equipped with a 'popanum'* **parma** *imitating such gladiators. (Photo: author)*

Many types of **hastae** *were in use during the Republican period. This relief (Diebner Is. 21), dating to the first years of the 1st century, shows a group of Roman marines equipped with shields and Montefortino helmets. The peculiar shape of the spearheads may be distinctive of the* **hasta navalis**. *(Photo: Deutschen Archäologische Instutut, Rome)*

Bronze figurine from Telamon, height 11.2 cm, usually dated to 250-150 and frequently stated to represent a Gaul at the Battle of Telamon in 225 (cf. Maule & Smith 47 n. 97). Von Vacano (1985, 140-142) has pointed out that the figure lacks the torques worn by Gauls and that the helmet is not Celtic. The two (sic) greaves and the tunic indicate that the figure represents a Roman soldier, possibly one of the hastati. (Photo: Museo Archaeologico, Florence; drawing after von Vacano)

The meaning of the Latin word *cohors* is uncertain (Keppie 235 n. 7). While dealing with the defeat of Hasdrubal, son of Gisco, by Publius Scipio, in 206, Polybius describes a combined arms column in which three *ilai* of cavalry precede 'the usual number' of *velites* (presumably the equivalent of three maniples), and three *speirai* of infantry. He then digresses that the Romans use the word 'cohort' for this formation (*syntagma*) of infantry. It has been suggested that Polybius is describing an *ad hoc* formation, which only became regularized by the Reforms of Marius (Keppie 67-8).

From time to time a number of cohorts could be grouped together for a specific tactical task, in which case they might be put under the charge of one of the tribunes. The first mention of a *cohors Romana* comes in 212 BC (Livy 25. 39. 1; Front. 2. 6. 2), and Bell (415) has suggested that the elder Scipios introduced it. Whatever its origins, the cohort does not seem to go far back into the 3rd century, and it has been suggested that in the early stages of its development the cohort con-

sisted of three maniples of any of the *ordines*, i.e. three maniples of *hastati* or of *principes*, as well as the later pattern of one maniple from each of the three *ordines* (Rawson 19 n. 20).

The maniple

Each cohort consisted of one maniple of *triarii*, numbering 60 men, one of *principes*, numbering 120, one of *hastati*, also numbering 120, plus 120 *velites*. The maniple is generally called a *sémaia*, though in one passage Polybius (6. 24. 8) uses the terms *sémaia* and *speira* indiscriminately to describe the maniple. The Latin term *manipulus* is clearly derived from *manus* (hand) which led to some rather fanciful etymological derivations in the ancient sources. Thus Plutarch (*Vit. Rom.* 8. 6) tells us that Romulus divided his forces into companies of 100 men, each led by a man carrying a standard consisting of a handful of grass and wood tied to a pole. In fact the word 'hand' has an early history as a term for a military subdivision and Herodotus uses the Greek word *cheir*

(hand) of a body of troops on a number of occasions (5. 72; 7. 20; cf. 7. 157). In the main, Polybius seems to use the word *speira* specifically to translate 'cohort', but sometimes he seems to use the term in place of *ordo*; that is, the line of battle – of *hastati*, *principes* or *triarii* (Walbank II 302).

It has frequently been suggested that the maniple was discontinued following the Marian reforms, but in fact it seems that it continued well into the Imperial period (Speidel 10). Aulus Gellius (*NA* 16. 4. 6) preserves a passage drawn from book six of the *De Re Militari* of L Cincius, a grammarian and antiquary active in the middle of the 1st century BC, describing the army after the Marian reforms, which mentions that in a legion there are 60 centuries, 30 maniples and ten cohorts.

The century

Each maniple was divided into two centuries, each commanded by a centurion. In battle the two centuries of the maniple would be drawn up side by side, the one on the right commanded by the senior centurion of the two (*centurio prior*) and the one on the left by the junior (*centurio posterior*). When the officers of the legion were being selected, all the *centuriones priores* were selected first, and all centurions holding this designation were superior in rank to every *centurio posterior*. The first centurion to be selected was the senior centurion of the legion, and he commanded the first century of the first maniple of the *triarii*. In later periods he was known as the *primus pilus prior*, though it is not known how far back this title went. Livy mentions the rank anachronistically in a number of references stretching back into archaic times, though his reference (42. 34. 11) to Spurius Ligustinus holding the rank shortly after 191 BC may be genuine.

The centuries of *hastati* and *principes* each numbered 60 men, and there is some evidence to indi-

Bronze figurine, probably Roman and, to judge by the 'designer stubble' beard, dating to the middle of the 1st century. Head, right arm and shoulder are pushed through the right arm hole to allow maximum freedom of movement. Although all weapons are broken away, it probably represents a soldier; perhaps one of the **antesignani**. *(Photo: Louvre)*

cate that each century was further divided into *contubernia*, or 'tent-parties' of six men each (Wheeler 312). Excavations of the Roman camp at Nobilior in Spain suggest that the centuries encamped in ten *contuburnia*, and this evidence is supported by Josephus (*BJ* 3. 124; 5. 48), who informs us that in the 1st century AD the Roman legion marched six abreast; presumably the legion is marching by *contuburnium* abreast.

The *principales*

The common soldiers of the century were known as *gregarii*. Each century had attached to it a number of staff, known as *principales*, who generally did not fight in the ranks of the century when it was drawn up for battle, but who were probably still counted as belonging to the *manipulares*. Polybius (6. 24. 2; cf. Festus s.v. *Optio*) tells us that each centurion appointed an *optio*. In the Imperial period the *optio* carried a large staff with which to beat men back into the ranks. He probably stood behind the century on the left-hand side

Third-century bronze statuette, height 9 cm, in the Villa Giulia, Rome. The dating is supported by the simple oval shape of the shield. It could represent a **princeps** *or a* **triarius,** *as both used the fighting-spear at this date. Note the* **Montefortino** *helmet and sword fastened on the right-hand side. The figure wears a simple tunic without mail cuirass or* **pectorale.** *(Drawing after Ausonia 2 (1907) p. 282 fig. 3; photo: Sopr. Arch. Etruria Méridionale)*

seo di Firenze
modelli, Milani,
d'arch. e num.
Greg., I, tav. X

(Speidel 24-5). Livy (8. 8. 18) mentions each centurion choosing a *subcenturio* during the Latin War (340–338 BC). He may be alluding to an early equivalent of the *optio*, or to a previous method of selecting the *centurio posterior* of the maniple.

Polybius also tells us (6. 24. 6) that the centurions chose two standard-bearers for each *speira* (here presumably with the meaning 'maniple'). Polybius has probably made a mistake. Varro (*Ling.* 5. 88; cf. Lucan 1. 296) tells us that in his time (he composed the *De Lingua Latina* in 47-5 BC) the maniple was the smallest sub-unit in the legion to have its own standard, and this was presumably also the case earlier on in the 2nd century. Perhaps Polybius' source stated that the senior centurion of the maniple chose a standard-bearer, but Polybius has misinterpreted the text to imply that both centurions in the maniple chose a standard-bearer. Each maniple would be drawn up in line with the standard. The standard-bearers would, therefore, be responsible for ensuring that the standards, and therefore the maniples, of each *ordo* (battle-line) were drawn up in line (Speidel 21).

The centuries of the Imperial legion also had another supernumerary officer called a *tesserarius*. He was responsible for passing on the watchword of the day, which was written on a small tablet (*tessera*) from which he derived his name. He was also responsible for selecting small sentry pickets and fatigue parties (Webster 117). Polybius (6. 34. 7 sq.) describes the way in which the watchword was circulated throughout the army, from the tent of the tribune, via the tenth maniple of each type of infantry, and so up through each maniple and back to the tribune's tent again. The man who was selected for this duty attended the tribune's tent each sunset (6. 34. 8). Presumably Polybius is describing a permanent appointment; in which case the rank of *tesserarius* existed as early as the 2nd century BC.

The Imperial century also had a *custos armorum*, who was in charge of the weapons and equipment, and who may also have been included among the *principales* (Breeze 267), though there is no evidence for the existence of this rank during the Republican period. This 'quartermaster-sergeant' or 'staff-sergeant' may well have been termed *hypéretés* in Greek, but the rank is not alluded to in this form in any of the Greek sources dealing with the army. Polybius (11. 22. 4) mentions that Publius Scipio, as soon as it was light, sent a message to the tribunes by his *hypéretai*. These *hypéretai* would seem to be the *beneficiarii*, who served as orderlies to the senior officers of the legion in Imperial times (Webster 118). Vegetius (2. 7) also mentions various types of trumpeter among the supernumeraries of the century of the Imperial army, and it is probable that the Republican maniple would have had its trumpeter too.

TACTICS

Manipular tactics are described by Livy (8. 8. 9-13). The maniples would normally be drawn up in three lines: *triarii* at the back; *principes* in the middle; and *hastati* at the front. This formation was known as the *triplex acies*, a term mentioned by Caesar (*Bell. Civ.* 1. 41. 2; *Bell. Gall.* 1. 24. 2;

Sealing taken from Roman Republican gem from Barcelona (Antike Gemmen in Deutschen Sammlungen I, 2 no. 1670), showing a Roman horseman riding down an infantryman, probably Roman, either a veles, *or perhaps an* antesignanus, *equipped with the lighter equipment sometimes given to these troops when operating with cavalry. (Photo: München, Staatliche Münzsammlungen)*

Bell. Afr. 60. 3). At Pharsalus, Caesar (*Bell. Civ.* 3. 89. 3) took cohorts out of his third line and constructed a fourth as a protection against the superior Pompeian cavalry. Crassus is mentioned as adopting a *duplex acies* in Aquitania (*Bell. Gall.* 3. 24. 1), and Caesar once had to draw up his army in *simplex acies* on account of the small number of troops available to him (*Bell. Afr.* 13. 2).

The maniples were not drawn up fighting 'shoulder to shoulder', but each maniple was bordered on either side by a space equal to that occupied by the maniple itself. The line of *principes* was staggered; their maniples were drawn up behind the spaces separating the maniples of the *hastati*, while the maniples of the *triarii* at the back were drawn up in line with the *hastati*. Spaces were also left between the three *ordines*. This 'chequerboard' formation, called *quincunx* by modern scholars, was the normal formation adopted by the maniples. At the Battle of Cannae, however, Varro abandoned the normal manipular formation; instead the maniples were drawn up in much closer order, and the battle-line as a whole was drawn up much more deeply than usual (Polyb. 3. 113. 3; cf. Livy 22. 47. 5). Nevertheless the *quincunx* formation, or variations on it, remained standard.

The 'popanum' shield seems to have staged a 'comeback' in the later years of the Republic. This Augustan funerary monument of an Italian settled in Thessalonike (Inscriptiones Graecae X, 2, 1. 378) shows a horseman dressed in a tunic and fringed cloak. His horse is shown in a 'window' at top right, and a juvenile, either his child or a slave, holds his cavalry **parma** *for him. (Photo: author)*

Pergamene terracotta representing a tray of temple offerings. Bossed temple cakes (popana) are shown, together with a pigeon, or some game bird. We might call Roman cavalry shields of this shape the 'popanum' type. (Photo after Töpperwien no. 598)

Each soldier occupied a space six feet square (Polyb. 18. 30. 8), allowing him to throw his *pila* and then wield his sword. We are not sure precisely how the ranks and files of the century were drawn up. Since the *contuburnium* numbered six men many modern scholars have suggested that the maniples of the *hastati* and *principes* were deployed 20 men wide and six deep, the *triarii* 20 wide and three deep (cf. Wheeler 305 n. 9). Each maniple would therefore have a frontage of 40 yards, and the legion 800 yards, allowing for the intervals in the *quincunx* formation. As the 2nd century progressed, the strength of the legion, and therefore of the individual maniples and centuries in it, gradually increased. The *hastati* were the

In 362 a chasm opened up in the Roman Forum. To expiate this evil portent Marcus Curtius rode into the gulf fully armed (Livy 7. 6. 3). This relief depicting the event, an Imperial copy of a Republican original, is in the Palazzo dei Conservatori. Note the 'popanum' shield decorated with a gorgoneion. (Photo: Deutschen Archäologische Instutut, Rome)

first, expanded to 200 per maniple, but the other *ordines* gradually followed. We may assume that the strength of the *contuburnia*, and thus the depth of each of the three ranks, rose accordingly. Thus, at Pharsalus, Pompey, whose legions each numbered 6,000, drew up his army in *triplex acies*, with each rank ten men deep (Frontin., *Strat.* 2. 3. 22).

The greatest exponent of manipular tactics during this period was Scipio Africanus. At the Battle of the Great Plains in Africa in 203 BC, Scipio drew up his army in the normal way (Polyb. 14. 8. 5), placing his maniples of *hastati* in front, behind them the *principes*, and at the back the *triarii*. Having engaged the enemy to the front with his *hastati*, Scipio redeployed the *principes* and *triarii* and attacked the Celtiberians in flank. Scipio thus 'prepares the way for the use of the reserve, as it is now understood' (Scullard 212). The next year, at the Battle of Zama, this time fighting Hannibal himself, Scipio suspected that the

Carthaginians were going to use their elephants to charge the legions in the centre of the Roman battle-line, so he drew up his army in a different variation of the *quincunx*, described by Polybius (15. 9. 7-9). In the front, the maniples of the *hastati* were drawn up with the usual gaps between each maniple. The ranks (*ordines* – here Polybius uses *speirai*) of the maniples of the *principes* and *triarii*, however, were not staggered behind them. Instead they were drawn up in line with the maniple in front. The normal spaces were also left between the three *ordines*. He filled the intervals between the front maniples of *hastati* with the *speirai* of *velites*. These harassed the elephants, but then withdrew through the passages opened to the rear, or through the gaps between the three *ordines*. Instead of disrupting the Roman formation, the Carthaginian elephants passed harmlessly through the gaps between the Roman maniples.

In general, however, the manipular battle was 'a corporal's battle'. Once the manipular lines had been drawn up, there was little chance for the general to intervene. Great reliance was placed on the initiative of junior commanders to exert local control on the battlefield. At the Battle of Pydna, a Pelignian officer, one Salvius, distraught by the inability of his troops to penetrate the Macedonian phalanx, snatched their standard and hurled it into the enemy ranks, encouraging his men to attack with redoubled fury rather than abandon their standard (Plut., *Vit. Aem. Paul.* 20). Hence the junior commanders, and especially the centurions – men with long years of continuous military experience – were considered to be the backbone of the army. One such individual was Spurius Ligustinus, whose military *curriculum vitae* is outlined by Livy (42. 34). He first served in 200 BC, and was promoted to centurion during the war against Philip of Macedon. He subsequently volunteered to serve in Spain as a private soldier, and was promoted to the rank of *centurio prior* of the first maniple of *hastati*. In subsequent campaigns he was appointed centurion *prior* of the first maniple of *principes*, and then was appointed *primus pilus* four times in the space of a few years. By 171 BC, over 50 years old by then, he had served 22 years, had been awarded for bravery 34 times and had received six civic crowns.

The *velites*

Battle commenced with the 120 *velites* of the cohort, drawn from the youngest and poorest troops (6. 21. 7), skirmishing in front of the 'chequerboard' formation. The role of the *velites* was to drive any enemy light-infantry from the battlefield, and then to attempt to disrupt the enemy battle-line. Prior to combat the *velites* would be stationed within the intervals between the maniples of the *hastati*. In 216 BC, at the Ebro, the Romans drew up their forces against Hasdrubal in *triplex acies*, with part of the *velites* stationed among the *antesignani* and part behind the standards (Livy 23. 29. 3). As light infantry, the *velites* were frequently singled out for special duties. Livy (26. 4. 4) describes how some young *velites* were picked out from all the legions on account of their swiftness of foot. On this occasion the *velites* rode into battle mounted on the hindquarters of the cavalry's horses. When they came into contact with the enemy cavalry, they would leap down

Denarius struck by C. Servilius commemorating some military exploit by one of his ancestors. The 'Greek' cavalry shield with its umbo and spine has replaced the 'popanum' shield. (Photo: author)

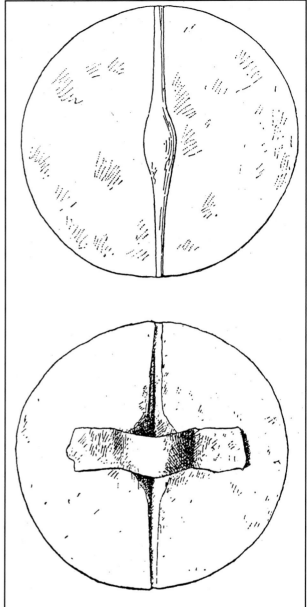

The shield-blazon on the shield of the previous figure is repeated as a coin-device on this **semiuncia** *(worth a twenty-fourth of an* **as***) struck in Republican Rome. It may thus have some significance beyond being merely the initial letter of Servilius' ancestor Marcius. (After Haeberlin pl. 40, 27)*

Right *The handle arrangement at the back of the 'Greek' type of Roman cavalry shield is unknown, but it may perhaps be reflected in this bronze votive miniature from Telamon. (Drawing after Milani 132 fig. 15)*

nimbly and fight on foot. This description from Livy has been held to indicate that the *velites* were created in 211, but it merely refers to the first time the *velites* were mounted. Roman light-armed troops had earlier been called *rorarii*, but during the 2nd century the term *velites* came into general use. The word *velites* occurs for the first time during Livy's account of the defeat of Regulus in 255 BC (1. 33. 9; cf. 2. 30. 1, 6).

Each *veles* carried a sword, javelins, and a round shield or *parma* three feet in diameter. Varro (*Ling.* 5. 115) tells us that the *parma* was so-called because from the centre it was even (*par*) in all directions. The javelin measured about 90-120 cm, with a 22.5 cm head, and was 2.5 cm thick. Examples of light javelin heads of this type have also been recovered from the Roman camps around Numantia (Connolly 131). Each man carried either seven (Livy 26. 4. 4) or five (Lucilius 7. 22) javelins. Livy (38. 21. 13) adds that, if compelled to fight hand-to-hand, the *velite* would transfer his javelins to his left hand and draw his Spanish sword.

Polybius doesn't tell us that the 120 *velites* attached to each cohort were organised into their own maniple. Rather he says that they were distributed equally among the *meré* (6. 25. 3). He previously used the term *meros* for the legion, but then uses it of the maniple. He then goes on to say (6. 24. 5) that they call each *meros* (i.e. subdivision?), *tagma* (legion?), *speira* (cohort) and *sémaia* (maniple). I don't understand what Polybius means. Most scholars have suggested that the *velites* were distributed among the other maniples in equal proportion (Connolly 129-130; Keppie 35 'for administrative purposes'). Certainly Livy (8. 8. 5) has the light-infantry distributed among the maniples when he describes the organization of the army during the Latin War (340-338). In combat, however, the *velites* would have nothing to do with the other maniples, for they opened battle by harassing the enemy, and then withdrew through the line of battle to form up once again, normally, behind the *triarii*. At the Battle of Ilipa, fought against the Carthaginians in Spain, in 206, Publius Scipio withdrew his *velites* through the intervals between his maniples but then redeployed them on the wings (Polyb. 11. 22. 10).

The *hastati*

When they had done what they could, the *velites* would withdraw through the gaps between the rearward maniples and leave the battlefield to the *hastati*. The *hastati* would throw their two *pila*, draw their swords, and then charge the enemy (cf. Caes., *Bell. Gall.* 1. 25. 2). The *hastati* were drawn from conscripts who were younger, and so presumably also poorer, than the *principes* or *triarii* (6. 21. 7) and may, therefore, have been less heavily armoured than the other two *ordines*. This seems to be reflected in the different tactical roles sometimes given to the *hastati*. At the Battle of Zama, following the defeat of the second rank of the Carthaginian army, when Scipio wished to re-form the line to attack the third rank, the *hastati* had to be recalled by trumpet as they were still pursuing the enemy (Polyb. 15. 14. 3).

The name *hastati* has caused some difficulties, for it literally means 'the *hasta*-men'. According to Polybius, however, they carried *pila*, and only the rear-rank men of the *triarii* carried *hastae*. Furthermore, troops fighting in the front rank might be thought of as being the last troops to be equipped with long spears rather than javelins. Consequently a number of complicated theories have been developed by modern scholars to explain this paradox. One would have the *ordines* of the legion originally fighting in a different order, with the *hastati* at the back. These theories are unnecessary, however, for, as Rawson (26) has pointed out, the earliest use of the word *hasta*, by Ennius (239-169) in his *Annales* (Skutch 446 frg.

In the late 15th century Maurice of Nassau attempted to recreate the Roman legionary from the descriptions of Livy and Polybius. The sword and target man carried a much larger shield than the sword and buckler man, and fought with a closed helmet and single greave on the leading left leg. (Photo: **Mars his feild** *or* **The Exercise of Arms** *(1625); second part entitled* **The Perfect Manner of Handling the Sword and Target Set forth in lively figures with the words of Command and Breife Instructions correspondent to every Posture.** *British Library)*

Reliefs from Dyrrhachion in Illyria. The gladiator on the right adopts the 'gladiator stance'; the leading leg thrust forward under the shield. The one on the left lunges forward with a rather dramatic sword-thrust: fighting left-handed, like the Emperor Commodus (Dio Cass. 72. 19), he is protected from head to toe by his enclosed helmet, **scutum** *and single greave. Note also the square* **pectorale** *decorated with a* **gorgoneion,** *the* **subligaculum** *(loin-cloth) with its armoured belt extended to protect the groin, the gauntlet (***manica***) and thong bindings on the arm. (After Heuzey & Daumet 383, pl. xxx)*

266), describes a throwing spear. Early Latin terms for throwing spears were not, it seems, clearly differentiated. Consequently Rawson has suggested that in the early 3rd century only the *hastati* of the first line were armed with throwing-spears – called *hastae velitares* – while the two back lines were armed with the long spears that were later called *hastae longae*. This suggestion is seemingly confirmed by Dionysius of Halicarnassus (20. 11. 2), who informs us that during the Pyrrhic War, probably the Battle of Beneventum in 275, those troops whom the Romans call *principes* fought in close order with 'cavalry spears' held in both hands. And

Plutarch's account of the Battle of Asculum in 279 (*Vit. Pyrrh.* 21. 6), presumably drawn from a contemporary source, has the Romans fighting with swords against the *sarisai* of the Epirote phalanx. It seems, then, that the front ranks of the Roman Army were already using the *pilum* and sword as early as 279. Polybius (1. 40. 12) also mentions javelins, presumably *pila*, in use at the Battle of Panormus in 250.

Roman Legionaries, Spain,
Second Punic War, 218-201 BC
1: Hastatus
2: Triarius
3: Veles

A

Cavalry, Thessaly, Second
Macedonian War, 200-197 BC
1,2: Cavalrymen
3: Veles

B

Roman Infantry, the Battle of Pydna, 168 BC
1,2: Infantrymen

C

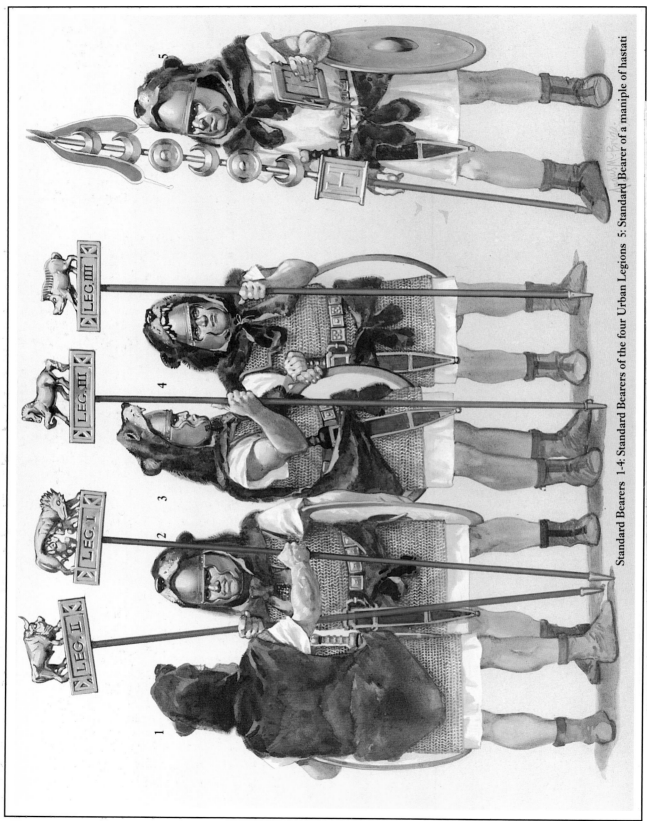

Standard Bearers 1-4: Standard Bearers of the four Urban Legions 5: Standard Bearer of a maniple of hastati

D

Mounted General in Wartime
1: General
2: Lictor
3,4: Scribes

E

Antesignani in combat with
Acheaen Cavalry, Acheaen War, 146 BC
1,3: Antesignani
2: Acheaen League Cavalryman

F

The Army towards the end of the period
1: Tribune
2: Eques
3,4: Infantry

The Army during the Jugurthine War, 110-105 BC
1: Centurion
2: Legionary
3: Cavalry Officer

H

Normally there were 1,200 *hastati* per legion (Polyb. 6. 21. 9), but according to Livy (33. 1. 2), Flamininus had 2,000 *hastati* in his legions in 197: thus 200 in each maniple rather than the normal 120. Flamininus' legions would therefore have had a total strength of 5,000 infantry. Flamininus used his *hastati*, travelling rapidly under cover, to frighten the ambassadors of the Boeotian League to come over to the Roman side. This was, again, a tactical situation suitable for less heavily armoured troops.

The *antesignani*

Livy (22. 5. 7) mentions that at the Battle of Lake Trasimene, in their confusion the Romans no longer fought in their lines of *principes*, *hastati* and *triarii*; nor did the ranks of the *antesignani* fight in front of the standards, with the rest brought up behind their standards; nor did they fight in their legion, cohort or maniple. We may conclude that the maniples of the *hastati*, fighting in front of the legion, were drawn up in front of their standards, while the maniples of the *principes* and *triarii* were drawn up behind their standards. For this reason, the *hastati* (and, presumably, the *velites* when they were still attached to the legionary cohorts) were also known as *antesignani*. Livy could be using the term *antesignani* anachronistically during his description of the Battle of Lake Trasimene, but the term seemingly goes back at least till 86 BC, for at the Battle of Chaironeia, Sulla deployed his army in *triplex acies*, leaving intervals through which to advance or withdraw his cavalry and light troops. The *postsignani*, who were in the second line, then fixed a line of stakes into the ground, and the line of *antesignani* were withdrawn through these stakes (Frontinus, *Strat.* 2. 3. 17).

After the Marian reforms, the *hastati*, though mostly fighting as regular infantry within the ranks, continued to play a specialist role as light infantry when the battlefield situation demanded. To some degree the absence of any light infantry within the legion in the post-Marian army (*velites* were no longer included in the legionary organization) placed increased burdens upon the *hastati*. This speculation can be supported by four passages illustrating Caesar's tactical improvisations during the civil war.

Relief from the Torre de San Magín, from the oldest stretch of city wall of Tarragona in Spain, probably 'Scipionic', erected by the Roman army during the last years of the 3rd century BC. The publisher (Grünhagen) explained the wolf-head badge on the umbo of the legionary shield held by Minerva as a native Spanish blazon of the god of war. (Photo: Deutschen Archäologische Instituts, Madrid)*

At the Battle of Ilerda in 49, Caesar (*BC* 1. 43) ordered *antesignani* to run out and capture an eminence of tactical importance on the plain in front of the town. We can assume that the *antesignani* were normally drawn up in the front ranks of the legion: the usual position of the *hastati* in fact. This initial skirmish was unsuccessful: more than 600 were wounded and 70 died, including Q. Fulginius, a centurion of the *hastati* of the first cohort of the XIV Legion. Somewhat later in the campaign Caesar (*BC* 1.57) detached 'the strongest men drawn from all the legions, *antesignani* and centurions' and gave them to Brutus to man a fleet against the Massilians.

The next year, in an engagement during the Dyrrachium campaign, 400 *antesignani* fought with great success mixed up with the cavalry (*BC* 3.75).

After Caesar's move into Thessaly, in view of the fact that his cavalry was far inferior to Pompey's, Caesar reinforced it with lightly-equipped young men drawn from the *antesignani* with arms selected for swiftness (*BC* 3. 84). Caesar had first developed these tactics fighting against the Germans under Ariovistus. He tells us (*Bell. Gall.* 1. 48) that the Germans trained infantrymen, as swift as they were brave, to fight with the cavalry, holding on to the manes of the horses. They would gather round any cavalryman who had been wounded, and could form a base upon which the horsemen could retire.

Putting this information together, it seems that during the civil wars, the *antesignani* – 'troops who fight before the standards' – were drawn from the younger men of the *hastati*. The two terms seemingly became interchangeable. The *antesignani* were frequently given lighter equipment than the rest of the legionaries, in order to carry out their task. The growth in the use of *hastati* as light infantry presumably coincided with the demise of the *velites* as an integral component of the legionary cohort.

In 107 the Roman general Marius had found himself unable to take the treasury of King Jugurtha, situated on top of a rocky hill not far from the River Muluccha. A Ligurian auxiliary found a path to the top of the rock while out gathering snails. Marius gave him five of the most agile of his trumpeters and buglers and four centurions, presumably along with their centuries. We are told (Sall. *Iug.* 94. 1) that the soldiers bared their heads and feet so as to be able to see better and climb more easily. They carried their swords and their shields on their backs, but took Numidian hide shields instead of their legionary ones, for they were lighter and made less noise when struck. These men were probably *antesignani*, and the passage illustrates how normal legionary equipment could be modified or abandoned according to the tactical demands of a situation.

The *antesignani* continued into the Imperial period. Inscriptions record that sets of equipment were held in store for them (Speidel 14). However, what these sets consisted of is not specified in any detail. According to Vegetius (2. 16), the *antesignani* used smaller or lighter armour than the other legionaries. Thus it seems that in the 2nd century BC the *hastati* would frequently wear less body-armour than the other ranks of the legion. Perhaps many wore no cuirass at all: Scipio led his legions out of camp on the five-day march preceding the Battle of the Great Plains in 203 'entirely in light order'. Polybius (14. 8. 1) might mean that Scipio ordered his legionaries to leave all their heavy baggage in camp, but more probably that they left some of their armour behind and wore a 'slimmed down' version of the legionary panoply.

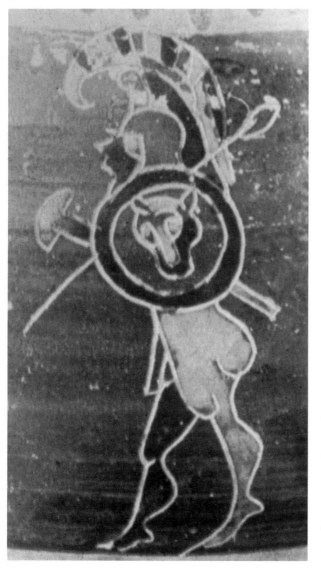

The wolf-head badge is also found in early Italian iconographic sources. Here it appears as a shield-bla-zon on an Etruscan olpe in the Villa Giulia Museum dating to the first half of the 6th century. (Photo: Sopr. Arch. Etruria Méridionale)

This statue probably represents the usurper L. Domitius Alexander dressed as the Roman god Silvanus with the lion skin of Hercules. Though dating to circa AD 310 it may demonstrate the original style of wearing an animal pelt over clothing adopted in early Rome: that is with both sets of paws tied at hip as well as at shoulder, a feature adopted in Plate D. (After von Heintze pl. 136)

The *principes*

If the *hastati* were unable to achieve victory, they would withdraw through the gaps in the maniples and re-form behind the *triarii*. The *principes*, in turn, would now throw their pair of *pila* (6. 23. 8), draw their swords, and charge the enemy. The 1,200 *principes* (6. 21. 9) were formed from men in the prime of life (6. 21. 7) with sufficient funds to provide themselves with body-armour. Consequently the order of the *principes* and *hastati* was sometimes reversed, presumably to avoid casualties among the lighter-armed *hastati*. In 181, during a campaign against the Ligurians, Lucius Aemilius placed the *principes* in the first line with the *hastati* in the second (Livy 40. 27. 6). As mentioned above, the *principes* still carried the *hasta longa* during the Pyrrhic Wars. At some point in the middle of the 3rd century they exchanged their *hastae* for *pila*.

The *triarii*

If the *principes* withdrew, the fighting came to the last line. The 600 *triarii* were composed of the oldest men (6. 21. 7, 9). Presumably the *triarii* were sufficiently wealthy to provide themselves with the mail cuirass. Under normal circumstances the *triarii* were kept in reserve, even if all other elements of the legion were engaged in an all-out attack. Livy (34. 15. 6) mentions how Cato led the *principes* and *hastati* of the second legion in an attack on the left gate of Emporiae in 195. While the *hastati* and *principes* were fighting, the *triarii* would sit, or rather kneel, beneath their standards, with the left leg bent forward, their shields leaning against their shoulders, and their spears thrust forward at an oblique angle (Livy 8. 8. 10; Varro, *Ling.* 5. 89). If formed up in *quincunx*, there would be gaps left in the last line. Livy (8. 8. 12) describes a manoeuvre in which the *triarii* would rise from the kneeling position, extend the frontage of each maniple so as to close the gaps in the line, and finally charge the enemy.

The *triarii* are first mentioned at the Battle of Cape Ecnomus in 256, which was fought between four legions manning the Roman fleet and the Carthaginians (Walbank, *Classical Review* 64 (1950) 10-11). The *triarii* were sometimes also termed *pilani* (Speidel 21); thus the senior centurion of the legion was called the *primus pilus*. Varro (*Ling.* 5. 89) incorrectly equates *pilani* with *pilum*, and speculates that the *triarii* had first used the *pilum*, and only later adopted the *hasta* as their principal weapon. Rather *pilani* seems derived from *pila*, a 'pillar' or 'column'; the *pilani* were troops stationed at the back of the column. When Polybius wrote (6. 23. 16), the *triarii* carried a single fighting-spear (*hasta longa*) rather than a pair of *pila*. Polybius (2. 33. 4) tells us that when the Roman Army contested the invasion of the Insubres in 223, the tribunes distributed the *hastae* of the *triarii* among the front ranks of the *hastati*. The intention was that their Celtic adversaries would blunt and bend their swords, slashing through the lines of spears in front of the Roman ranks, before coming to grips with the Romans in hand-to-hand fighting. As the 2nd century progressed the *triarii* gradually exchanged their *hastae* for *pila*.

During the Third Macedonian War (171-168 BC) the strength of the legion frequently rose to 6,000 or 6,200. This implies that, as the strength of Flamininus' legions rose to 5,000 when the maniples of the *hastati* were expanded to 200, the maniples of the *principes* and/or *triarii* were expanded later. The strengths of the various *ordines* in a 6,200-strong legion can only be guessed, but if we deduct 1,200 for the *velites*, then the ten maniples of *hastati* and *principes* might have numbered 200 each, and the ten maniples of *triarii* could have numbered 100. Presumably the frontage of 20 was retained for all the maniples; otherwise the *quincunx* formation would not have fitted together, and so the maniples of 200 men would have a depth of ten ranks.

OTHER ARMS

Cavalry

The *equites*, or 'knights', formed the highest echelon of Roman society. Known as *equites equo publico*, their numbers stood at 1,800 and their horses were supplied and maintained by the state. An *eques* might lose his status at an inspection (*recognitio*) through unworthy conduct, because his horse was inadequately cared for, or if found physically unfit for cavalry service. The status of *eques equo publico* became increasingly honorific.

Three hundred cavalry were assigned to each

This denarius, struck in Marseilles by C. Valerius Flaccus while Proconsul in Gaul in 82 (Keppie 67), shows the legionary eagle standard introduced by *Marius, flanked by standards marked P for the* **principes** *and H for the* **hastati.** *(Photo: Bibliothèque Nationale, Paris)*

Statue from Herculaneum in the National Museum, Naples, showing a member of the Balbus family wearing the military dress of a proconsul or praetor. Though Augustan, the statue probably represents the dress of a military commander of the later Republican period reasonably accurately. (Photo: Deutsches Archäologisches Instututs, Rome)

legion (Polyb. 6. 20. 9) - a total of 1,200 horsemen. If more than four legions were raised, their numbers could be supplemented by citizens supplying their own horses: *equites equis suis merentes* or *equites equo privato*. The organization and equipment of the legionary cavalry is described in Polybius 6. 25. The cavalry was divided into ten *ilai* (*turmae*) of 30 men, each containing three *decuriones*, one *decurio* commanding the *turma* as a whole. The *decuriones* themselves each appointed an *optio*, though later on the tribunes appointed the *optiones* themselves (Varro, *Ling.* 5. 91). Presumably the *turma* was drawn up in three ranks of ten, each rank having its *decurio* on the right and its *optio* on the left.

Polybius tells us that the Roman cavalry had once been lightly equipped, but were now more heavily armed and wore cuirasses. They had substituted their native weapons for ones borrowed from the Greeks. Their spears had been too slender and pliant to allow them to aim an accurate blow: they had tended to vibrate, and they broke too easily. When they did break, since the spears had no butt-spikes, they couldn't aim a second blow. Consequently the cavalry were now using Greek cavalry-spears.

The shield they had formerly made use of, Polybius (6. 25. 7) tells us, was made of ox-hide, and was similar in shape to the *popanum*, 'the round, bossed cake used in sacrifices'. They were not firm enough to be used effectively in the attack, and once wet, their leather covering tended to peel off. Consequently the Romans started to copy Greek cavalry shields. Polybius probably has in mind the large, round cavalry shields with a central boss and a spine reinforcing the shield. Indeed one can see Roman cavalry using Greek

shields of this type on coins of Republican date, but they never supplanted the traditional 'popanum' shield entirely, for these too continue to be shown on coins of Augustus and on funerary monuments of the same date (cf. Bishop & Coulston, frontispiece).

Allied contingents

The Roman Army increasingly relied on allied contingents for its cavalry and light infantry. Each Roman army was usually accompanied by an equal number of allied infantry, but by three times as many cavalry (Polyb. 6. 26. 7). The consuls would appoint 12 prefects to command the allies (*praefecti sociorum*), and of the six appointed to each consular army, three would fight on each wing commanding the allied contingents (cf. Polyb. 6. 34. 3). Many of these allied cohorts may have been equipped in the same way as the Roman legionary cohorts, banded together into tens in an *ala sociorum*, the equivalent of a legion, each commanded by one of the six *praefecti sociorum* appointed by the consuls (Keppie 22). The precise details varied from campaign to campaign. For example, in the mobilization of 171 for the war against Perseus (Livy 42. 35. 4-6) the four urban legions were mobilized and the praetor Gaius Sulpicius Galba chose four military tribunes from the senate as their commanders. As these legions were divided between two consular armies, only two fought at Pydna. The 'Allies of Latin Name' supplied 15,000 infantry and 1,200 cavalry, while

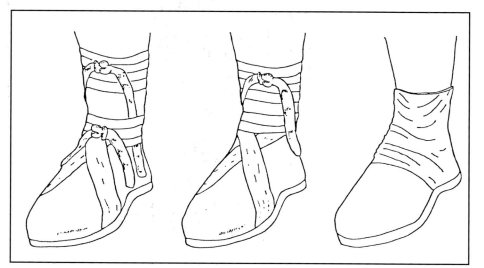

Three types of Roman boot denoting social rank in the Imperial period. Left, the **calceus patricius**, *worn only by patricians; centre, the* **calceus senatorius**, *worn only by members of Senate; right, the* **calceus equester**, *restricted to members of the Equestrian Order. (Drawing after Goette 451 fig. 35b)*

Bronze figurine of a Roman lictor, Augustan in date, in the British Museum. Note the bound fasces, *the equestrian boots, and the full toga worn in times of peace. (Photo: author)*

the Ligurians supplied 2,000 infantry. The Cretans and Numidians also supplied troops, and elephants were attached to the army.

Units of allied light infantry were organized into cohorts along Roman lines. Pompey had two cohorts of 600 slingers in Greece (Caesar, *Bell. Civ.* 3. 4. 3). Cohorts of allied light infantry increasingly supplemented or replaced the legionary *velites* in the later 2nd century. As the size of armies increased, so did the demand for citizen manpower. It is generally accepted that the Roman military machine was beginning to run out of available manpower by the end of the 2nd century, though this view has been challenged (Evans 20; Rich). It became increasingly difficult to find sufficient citizen manpower from the *adsidui* alone to fill the three *ordines*. Indeed, in 107 Marius was forced to extend recruitment to the *proletarii*. The probable result of all this was that fewer and fewer citizens were available to serve as *velites*.

There was probably a second, tactical, reason for the demise of the *velites*. The conquest of the western Mediterranean, and particularly of Spain, involved the Romans in irregular combat with various tribal enemies, who could field formidably efficient light infantry. Against these troops the *velites* were often ineffective, and demand increased for more efficient missile troops with better weapons who could keep the enemy at a distance (Bell 419).

In 133 at Numantia, Scipio Aemilianus deployed archers and slingers interspersed not only with his cohorts, but even with his centuries (Front. 4. 7. 27). These troops may have been the archers and slingers brought over by Jugurtha with 12 elephants in the winter of 134 (Bell 419 n. 106).

In 109 Metellus adopted a similar expedient at the Battle of Muthul during the Jugurthine War, dispersing archers and slingers between the maniples of his line (Sallust, *BJ* 49. 6). Bell (416) noted that two of the *legati* of Metellus, Marius and P. Rutilius Rufus, had served under Scipio in the Numantine War, and it is probable that these two individuals were instrumental in spreading the new tactical ideas.

The practice of interspersing missile troops among the legionary cohorts continued into the 1st century. During his campaign against the Parthians, Antony arranged for his javelinmen and slingers to sally out through the lines of his legionaries (Plut., *Vit. Ant.* 41. 4-5). Light-armed troops could also be dispersed among the cavalry (Caes., *Bell. Afr.* 60).

The traditional view is that the legions were deprived of their *velites* by the Marian reforms. Bell (421-2) has pointed out that although *velites* had wholly disappeared by the time of Caesar, the term does occur sporadically in sources from the earlier part of the 1st century. For example, Frontinus (*Strat.* 2. 3. 17), in describing Sulla's dispositions at Orchomenos, mentions how the *velites* and light-armed troops discharged their javelins at the oncoming Pontic chariotry. Bell suggests that Lucullus, who made little use of light troops, may have been more responsible than anyone else for the demise of the legionary *velites*. Perhaps, though, we should not assume that our sources are using the term *velites* in the restricted meaning of legionary *velites*, but rather to describe allied cohorts equipped in the same way as the legionary *velites*.

Sallust (*BJ* 105. 2) describes how Marius sent Sulla to meet the Mauritanean King Bocchus with a guard of horsemen, Balearic slingers, archers, and a cohort of Paelignians '*cum velitaribus armis*'. Thus the term may have lingered on after the disestablishment of the legionary *velites*. In the groundplan of Camp III at Reneiblas near Numantia in Spain (Keppie 46-7), which is thought to have been constructed by Q. Fulvius Nobilior in 153/2, there is no room for any *velites* in the accepted reconstruction.

THE ROMAN LEGION IN BATTLE

The Roman Republican army was principally an infantry army. Roman commanders were, however, keenly aware of the value of cavalry. In 184 Cato held the office of censor at Rome, together with one Valerius, and attempted to rid the *equites* of all unfit to serve; presumably to restore the military utility of the institution. It was probably at this time too that Cato attempted to persuade the Senate to raise the size of the *equites* from 1,800 to 2,200 (Astin 81-2). Cato's efforts seem to have been unsuccessful, for the last references to Roman Republican citizen cavalry (for which I thank B. Rankov) concern the Battle of Vercellae in 102, when the younger M. Aemilius Scaurus retreated from before the Cimbri whilst serving as an *eques* (Valerius Maximus 5. 8. 4; Frontinus, *Strat.* 4. 1. 13). Subsequently the Republican Army seemingly relied exclusively on allied cavalry.

Campania was particularly important for both recruits and remounts. Following the Battle of Cannae, the Romans were concerned to retain control of Campania, capable of supplying 4,000 cavalry (Livy 23. 5. 15). Lucilius, who served in the cavalry under Scipio during the Numantine War in 134/3, mentions Campanian horses in a fragmentary passage drawn from his *Satires* (506-8).

Rome frequently enjoyed a considerable superiority in cavalry during her battles with Macedonian and Greek armies, and this was a principal factor in her victories. Under Philip and Alexander, the Macedonian state had been capable of raising large numbers of cavalry, principally because of the 'Companion' system, deliberately supported by land-grants and by other devices, which extended the potential pool of propertied horse-owning cavalry recruits. Subsequent social change in Macedonia, coupled with lack of state finances, served to diminish the numbers of cavalry available for recruitment by the state. During their wars with the Romans, the Macedonians were rarely able to raise more than a few hundred horsemen. Consequently the Macedonians came to rely more and more on their phalanx to achieve victory, but they rarely had sufficient cavalry available to secure its flanks.

We may compare the success of the Roman swordsmen against the phalanx to the success of the Biscayan sword-and-buckler men in Spanish service over the Swiss pikemen of Louis XII at the Battle of Cerignola in 1503. Contemporary military pundits, however, while directly comparing the sword-and-buckler men to the Roman legionaries and advocating their use, recognised that in the open field they could not stand against cavalry. Had the Macedonians of the 2nd century possessed an effective cavalry arm to protect the flanks of their phalanx and to attack the legions, the battles of the Macedonian Wars may have turned out very differently. Thus, at the Battle of Magnesia, Antiochus the Great managed to break through the lines of the left-hand Roman legion with his cavalry *agéma* and cataphracts (Bar-Kochva 170; cf. Briscoe 355).

Terracotta sarcophagus, dated to the first quarter of the 1st century (Vacano 1960) showing a club, greaves, and shields decorated with geometric shield-devices. (Photo: Museo Archeologico, Florence)

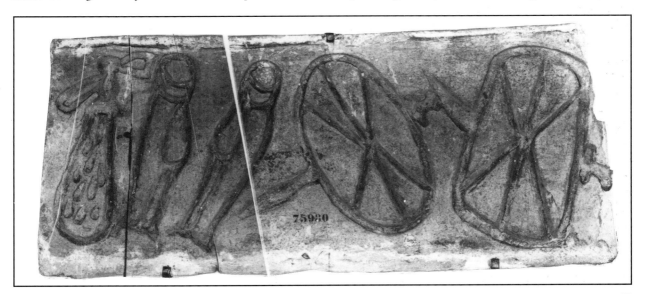

91

Another significant factor in Rome's victories was the brutality of her soldiery. This feature might be explained as arising from the constant wars in which Rome became involved during this period, but these wars only served to exacerbate an already deeply rooted predisposition towards violence. The institutionalization of violence, even in the gladiatorial pastimes of Roman society, fostered a thirst for violence in all forms of social activity, and more particularly a lust for war. Brutality and massacre were hallmarks of Roman methods of warfare, and the capture of a Greek city was normally followed by mass rape and massacre from which even the dogs were not spared (Harris 51-3, 263-4). The prospect of rape, violence and plunder in a foreign country have always been potent weapons in the armoury of the recruiting sergeant. In the militarized society of Republican Rome the blandishments of sex and violence abroad helped greatly in diverting the attention of the poor from the appalling social injustices of the Roman political system. Thus love of violence was not simply an unsavoury excrescence of the Roman social system, it was the gel which held it together. This brutality tended to paralyze the capacity of Rome's enemies to resist her effectively.

Perhaps the most important factor in Roman success was, however, her superiority in manpower. When Hannibal invaded Italy with less than 20,000 men, Polybius (2. 24. 16) tells us that the Romans and their allies were capable of mustering, at least on paper, 700,000 foot and 70,000 horse (cf. Brunt). It was Rome's capability to mobilize such huge armies which defeated Macedon, rather than any innate superiority of the Roman military system. No matter how many armies the incompetence of Roman military commanders might lose, there was always a near-inexhaustible reservoir of manpower to draw on. The first years of the Third Macedonian War saw many Roman reverses, but these didn't matter; all that mattered was the last battle.

Bibliography

M.E. Agnew, 'A Numbered Legion in a Fragment of the Elder Cato', *American Journal of Philology* 60 (1939) pp. 214-219

G. Alföldy, *Noricum* (1974) pl. 20

A.E. Astin, *Cato the Censor* (1978)

R. Bianchi Bandinelli, *Les Étrusques et l'Italie avant Rome* (1973)

R. Bianchi Bandinelli & M. Torelli, *L'Arte dell'Antichité Classica 2 Etruria, Roma* (1976)

B. Bar-Kochva, *The Seleucid Army. Organization and Tactics in the Great Campaigns* (1976)

M.J.V. Bell, 'Tactical Reform in the Roman Republican Army' *Historia* 14 (1965) pp. 404-422

M.C. Bishop & J.C.N. Coulston, *Roman Military Equipment from the Punic Wars to the Fall of Rome* (1993)

R. Bloch, *Tite-Live et les premiers siècles de Rome* (1965)

D.J. Breeze in *Bonner Jahrbücher* 174 (1974)

J. Briscoe, *A Commentary on Livy books XXXIV - XXXVII* (1981)

P.A. Brunt, *Italian Manpower 225 B.C.–A.D. 14* (1971)

P.G. Calligas, 'Roman Helmets in Greece' *Athens Annals in Archaeology* 18 (1985) pp. 161-164.

P. Connolly, *Greece and Rome at War* (1981)

S. Diebner, *Aesernia-Venafrum. Untersuchungen zu den römischen Steindenkmälern zweier Landstädte Mittelitaliens* (1979)

C. van Driel-Murray, 'New light on old tents' *Journal of Roman Military Equipment Studies* 1 (1990) pp. 109-137

M. Eichberg, *Scutum* (1987)

J.K. Evans, *American Journal of Ancient History* 5 (1980) p. 20

W. Froehner, *Collection J. Gréau. Catalogue des bronzes antiques* (1885)

N. Fuentes, 'The Roman Military Tunic' in ed. M. Dawson, *Roman Military Equipment. The Accoutrements of War. Proceedings of the Third Roman Military Equipment Research Seminar* (1987) pp. 41-75

E. Gabba, *Republican Rome, The Army and the Allies* (1976)

H.R. Goette, 'Mulleus - Embas - Calceus: Ikonografische Studien zu Römischem Schuhwerk' *Jahrbuch des Deutschen Archäologischen Instituts* 103 (1988) pp. 401-464

W. Grünhagen, 'Bemerkungen zum Minerva-Relief in der Stadtmauer von Tarragona'

Limestone base from an honorific monument erected for Sextus Appuleius, consul in 29 (Diebner Is. 28). Note the 1st century infantry shield, dateable by its 'excised' top and bottom, decorated with a geometric pattern, and a 'popanum' shield decorated with a lion's head. (Photo: Deutschen Archäologische Instututs, Rome)

Madrider Mitteilungen 17 (1976) pp. 209-225

E.J. Haeberlin, *Aes Grave* (1910)

J. Harmand, *L'Armée et le Soldat à Rome de 107 à 50 avant notre ère* (1967)

W.V. Harris, *War and Imperialism in Republican Rome* (rev. ed. 1985)

H. von Heintze, *Römische Kunst* (1969)

L. Heuzey & H. Daumet, *Mission archéologique de Macédoine* (1876)

H. Kähler, *Der Fries vom Reiterdenkmal des Aemilivs Pauvlvs in Delphi (= Monumenta Artis Romanae V,* 1965)

L. Keppie, *The Making of the Roman Army, From Republic to Empire* (1984)

W. Kimmig, 'Ein Keltenschild aus Aegypten' *Germania* 24 (1940) pp. 106-111

Peter Kränzle, *Die zeitliche und ikonographische Stellung des Frieses der Basilica Aemilia* (1991)

Q.F. Maule & H.R.W. Smith, *Votive Religion at Caere: Prolegomena* (1959)

E. Meyer, 'Das Römische Manipularheer, seine Entwicklung und seine Vorstufen' in his *Kleine Schriften* II (1924) pp. 193-329

L.A. Milani, *Studi e materiali di Archeologia e Numismatica I, I* (1899)

John Paddock, 'Some changes in the manufacture and supply of Roman helmets under the late Republic and early Empire' in *The Production and Distribution of Roman Military Equipment,* ed. M.C. Bishop (1985) pp. 142-159

H.M.D. Parker, *Roman Legions* (1958) pp. 9-20

P. Pensabene, 'Sur un fregio Fittile e un Ritratto Marmoreo da Palestrina nel Museo Nazionale Romano' in *Miscellanea Archeologica Tobias Dohrn dedicata* (1982) pp. 73-88

E. Rawson, 'The Literary Sources for the Pre-Marian Army' *Papers of the British School at Rome* 39 (1971) pp. 13-31

J.W. Rich, 'The Supposed Manpower Shortage of the Later Second Century BC' *Historia* 32 (1983) 287-331

H. Russell Robinson, *The Armour of Imperial Rome* (1975)

H.H. Scullard, *Scipio Africanus in the Second Punic*

War (1930)

O. Skutsch, *The Annals of Q. Ennius* (1985)

A.N. Sherwin-White, *The Roman Citizenship²* (1973)

M. Speidel, *The Framework of the Roman legion: the fifth annual Caerleon lecture in honorem Aquilae Legionis II Augustae* (1992)

J. Suolahti, *The Junior Officers of the Roman Army in the Republican Period* (1955)

R.J.A. Talbert, *The Senate of Imperial Rome* (1984)

L. Ross Taylor, *Roman Voting Assemblies* (1966)

E. Töpperwein, *Terrakotten von Pergamon* (= *Pergamenische Forschungen 3*, Berlin 1976)

M. Torelli, *Typology and Structure of Roman Historical Reliefs* (1982)

Treloar, *Classical Review* 21 (1971) pp. 3-5

O.W. von Vacano *Römischer Mitteilungen* 67 (1960) p. 74 pl. 24, 2

O.W. von Vacano, *Gli Etruschi a Talamone, etc.* (1985)

O.W. von Vacano, *Der Talamonaccio. Alte und Neue Probleme* (1988)

F.W. Walbank, *A Historical Commentary on Polybius* I (1956) – III (1979)

G. Webster, *The Roman Imperial Army³* (1985)

E.L. Wheeler, 'The Legion as Phalanx' *Chiron* 9 (1979) pp. 303-318

L.M. Wilson, *The Clothing of the Ancient Romans* (1938)

THE PLATES

A: Roman legionaries, Spain, Second Punic War
Roman legionaries in Spain during the closing stages of the Second Punic War. The oblong shield shown on the sculpture of Minerva from Tarragona has been used for the *hastatus* (**A1**) and the *triarius* (**A2**). The head of a she-wolf shown in the relief may be a Roman legionary blazon. The *hastatus* wears a *pectorale*, decorated with stylised musculature as was the earlier practice, while the *triarius* wears a mail cuirass, here secured at the chest with a clasp, in the Celtic fashion, rather than by shoulder guards. The single greaves worn by both figures are based on the figurine once in the Collection Gréau. Polybius (6. 22) informs us that the *velites* (**A3**) wore 'a simple helmet', which

they sometimes covered with the skin of a wolf or some other animal. He does not tell us the *velites* wore a complete wolf-skin. The 'simple' helmet worn by **A2** is of the Italo-Corinthian type. The javelins follow the reconstructions of Connolly (131), which are based on surviving 2nd-century examples.

We have no information on the appearance of the Spanish sword, scabbard or sword-belt, nor of the style of boot worn by Roman legionaries during this period, so relevant details in the reconstructions throughout this book are speculative. Tunics of a natural off-white colour, as worn during the Imperial period (Fuentes), have been restored.

B: Cavalry, Thessaly, Second Macedonian War
Two cavalrymen on reconnaisance in Thessaly during the Second Macedonian War, gathering information from a *veles*. **B1**, based on the Curtius relief, carries a shield of the 'popanum' variety. **B2**, based on the Servilius coin, carries a 'Greek' shield with a central spine. Both figures wear the cavalry cloak (*sagum*), which is known to have been a heavy cloak of very dark, practically black colour; presumably made of extremely dark brown natural wool, and often worn as mourning dress (Wilson 105). Plutarch (*Vit. Crass.* 23. 1) tells us that Crassus put on a black cloak instead of his general's red cloak on the eve of the Battle of Carrhae in 53; this act was interpreted as a bad omen by the troops. Presumably Crassus had put on the cloak he had worn previously as a cavalry officer.

The tunics have been restored as bleached white, with a narrow purple stripe running down from both shoulders to the hem – a distinction which seems to have been limited to the *equites* during the Republican period. All other colours in the plate are arbitrary. **B2** wears boots of the style which later became standard dress for the equestrian order, while **B1** wears boots related to the later type which denoted members of the senator-

Opposite *Detail of a 1st century Etruscan cinerary urn from Volterra (Bandinelli fig. 372). Note the boots, precursors to the later 'senatorial' type, and the ornamental spearhead: both most probably insignia of rank. (Photo: Museo Guarnacci)*

ial order. The horse furniture is decorated with silver *phalerae*, which Livy (22. 52. 5) mentions being captured in large numbers by Hannibal after the Battle of Cannae.

B3 uses the same equipment as **A3**. The custom of wearing the mask of an animal over the helmet was seemingly derived from hunting practice, for Grattius (*Cynegeticon* 340) mentions hunters' caps made from badger. Thus the mask of a badger has been restored. The shield design is based on a sculpture from the Basilica Aemilia (Kränzle p. 120), but the colours used are arbitrary.

C: Roman Infantry, the Battle of Pydna, 170BC

Roman infantrymen, based on the Aemilius Paulus Monument at Delphi, versus the Macedonian Chalcaspides regiment at the Battle of Pydna. Greaves have been entirely abandoned. Some figures wear the familiar mail cuirass, but others wear the Italian muscle-cuirass, which can be recognized by its lack of shoulder-guards. **C1** has been restored with a helmet of Italo-Corinthian type, possibly suggested by one damaged head on the monument, while **C2** has been restored with the more familiar Montefortino type.

D: Standard Bearers of the four Urban Legions

Pliny (*HN* 10. 5. 16) tells us that Marius gave the Roman legions their eagle standards during his second consulship in 104. Prior to that the eagle had been their first badge along with four others: the wolf, the minotaur, the horse and the boar, which went before the different ranks (*ordines*). It is possible to suppose Pliny is referring to the *ordines* of the *triarii*, *principes*, and *hastati*, but four standards does not divide easily into three *ordines*. Thus it seems preferable to assume that the four additional legionary badges mentioned by Pliny belonged to the original four urban legions. **D1-D4** show the standard-bearers of the four urban legions standing in front of the walls of an Italian sanctuary precinct. Over their mail cuirasses they wear bearskins, and at their belts they suspend *parmae* which are similar to those used by the *velites*. **D5** shows a standard-bearer of a maniple of *hastati*, consequently he is not wearing body-armour.

E: A General in Wartime

E1, based on the statue of Balbus, represents a mounted general of senatorial rank. During this period consuls would frequently command armies. In peacetime consuls would wear a white toga and tunic decorated with purple stripes and white boots (Lydus, *de magistr.* 1. 32. 1); in times of war the toga was laid aside for the military cloak (*paludamentum*). Pliny (*HN* 22. 3. 3) mentions that the scarlet dye of the 'coccum' was reserved to colour the *paludamenta* of generals. This is confirmed by Silius Italicus (4. 518, 17.395-8), who mentions Roman generals dressed in scarlet with scarlet cloaks, although other sources mention purple (Caes., *Bell. Afr.* 57; Appian, *Pun.* 66) or crimson (Plut., *Vit. Crass.* 23. 1) cloaks. Literary sources mention consuls and other senators wearing the 'senatorial' or 'patrician' boot coloured either black or scarlet, while further texts mention the black thongs which bound the boot up (Talbert 219). We may presume that the boot itself was scarlet, but with black. The sole of the boot has been restored as black thongs. His horse has scarlet horse furniture decorated with *gold phalerae*, which were insignia normally awarded only to military commanders, including consuls (Bloch p. 108).

E2: Before the general march two of his 12 lictors. The *fasces* were a bundle of rods and an axe, symbolizing the magistrate's ability to inflict either corporal or capital punishment, bound together with a red band (Lydus, *De magistr.* 1. 32. 4). Various sources mention lictors laying aside their short togas (Cic., *In Pis.* 55) for *paludamenta* in times of war (Livy 41. 10. 5, 45. 39. 11; Varro, *Ling.* 7. 37), while others mention lictors dressed in red (Silius Italicus 9. 419; cf. Appian, *Pun.* 66). White *paludamenta* wrapped round the waist over red tunics have been restored following a polychrome frieze (Pensabene), as have the ivory crescents worn on the boot as a badge of rank. Also shown are the general's scribes, based on a relief from Gamlitz (Alföldy pl. 20). As non-military personnel they don't wear their tunics girt high up above the knees, ready for action. For the tent, see C. van Driel-Murray.

F: Combat

Roman *antesignani* (**F1, 3**) in combat with cavalry

of the Achaean League (**F2**). The *antesignani* are equipped with small swords and shields in place of their full legionary equipment. They attack both riders and steeds, striking up at the bellies of the horses and at the legs of the riders. The Achaean cavalryman is based on a statue of Polybius and a polychrome terracotta from Corinth.

G: The Army towards the end of the period

Based on the 'Altar of Domitius Ahenobarbus', representing the Army towards the end of this period. **G1** represents a Roman senior officer. His tunic is bleached, for Tacitus (*Hist.* 2. 89) tells us that the tribunes and senior centurions of Vitellius' army wore bleached garments (*candida veste*) during their entry into Rome in AD 69. He wears a bronze muscle-cuirass, helmet and greaves, but the colours of all other details, including the white leather groin-flaps outlined in red, are arbitrary. A decorative head has been restored to his spear, of the type used as badges of rank during the Imperial period. The helmet type is unclear from the relief, but it could be of 'Boeotian' type with cheek-pieces.

G2 wears the *sagum* and white purple-striped tunic of an *eques*. Equestrian boots have also been restored to this figure. His helmet, of 'Boeotian' type, has a yellow plume. Arrian (*Ars Tactica* 34.4) mentions Roman cavalry wearing yellow plumes some 250 years later, but we have no idea when this became standard practice. A gold finger-ring was the sign of an *eques* in the late Republic (Bloch 107).

G3 and **G4**: In accordance with the Kasr el-Harit shield, the rim, spine and boss of the shield are left felt without metal reinforcement. One figure only, it seems, wears a version of the 'Montefortino' helmet, which must by now have become standard, thus the helmets worn by the other figures may be due to artistic licence.

H: The Army during the Jugurthine War

Centurion of a cohort of Sabine auxiliary infantry, perhaps during the Jugurthine War. Some Sabine communities may not have received Roman citizenship, and thus continued to supply allied contingents until the early 1st century (Sherwin-White 206-7). As a centurion he wears a bleached white tunic and a distinctive red crest. **H2** shows a legionary carrying a shield decorated with a geometric pattern. Such patterns, probably based on Gallic prototypes, are shown on a number of archaeological monuments of the period. The rest of the equipment he uses is derived from the Domitius Ahenobarbus altar. **H3** shows a cavalry officer. The shield is based on that shown on the Sextus Appuleius monument, though the colours are hypothetical.

CHRONOLOGY

44 BC: Conspirators assassinate the Dictator, Gaius **Julius Caesar**. Marcus Antonius, a close friend of Caesar, takes control and inflames public opinion against the conspirators, forcing Brutus and Cassius, the prime movers, to flee Italy.

The great-nephew of the Dictator, Gaius Julius Caesar Octavianus, succeeds in gaining the support of the Senate against Antonius and emerges as his rival for power.

43 BC: Octavianus defeats Antonius at Mutina and the latter retreats across the Alps to Gallia Narbonensis. Octavianus becomes reconciled with Antonius later in the year, and together with Marcus Aemilius Lepidus, who replaced Caesar as chief priest, they form the Second Triumvirate[1].

42 BC: Octavianus and Antonius engage and defeat Brutus and Cassius at Philippi in Macedonia. Both conspirators commit suicide.

40 BC: Octavianus and Antonius agree to divide the rule of the Roman world between them and Antonius marries Octavia, the sister of Octavianus.

36 BC: Antonius campaigns against the Parthians.

33 BC: Mistrust and rivalry between the two leaders worsens, largely as a result of Antonius' association with the Egyptian queen, Cleopatra.

32 BC: Antonius formally divorces Octavia in favour of Cleopatra, and the breech between the two leaders becomes irreconcilable.

The grave stele of Caius Valerius Crispus, a legionary of Legio VIII Augusta, who served during the first half of the 1st century AD—see colour plate C1. (In the collection of the Stadtisches Museum, Wiesbaden)

[1] An officially constituted dictatorial committee.

31 BC:	Antonius and Cleopatra are defeated in a naval engagement off Actium and retreat to Egypt.
30 BC:	Octavianus takes Egypt and both Antonius and Cleopatra commit suicide. Octavianus becomes the effective ruler of the Roman world.
27 BC:	Octavianus takes the titles 'Imperator' and '**Augustus**', and becomes the first Roman Emperor.
25 BC:	Galatia is annexed as a Roman province.
16–15 BC:	Tiberius and Nero Drusus, stepsons of Augustus, annexe the provinces of Noricum and Raetia.
12–9 BC:	The territory north of Illyricum is annexed by Tiberius as the province of Pannonia.

Birth of Christ

AD 9:	Three legions under P. Quinctilius Varus—the XVIIth, XVIIIth and XIXth—are destroyed in the Teutoburg Forest: an extremely serious loss of men and equipment which forestalls Roman intentions of annexation across the Rhine.
AD 14:	Augustus dies and the Rhine and Pannonian legions mutiny. His successor, **Tiberius** Cladius Nero, quells the revolt and army conditions are improved to avoid further trouble.
AD 14–16:	Germanicus undertakes three campaigns against the Germans east of the Rhine and reaches the River Elbe, but no permanent presence is established.
AD 37:	Tiberius dies and is succeeded by the insane Gaius Caesar, nicknamed '**Caligula**'. Gaius Caesar may have been a victim of lead poisoning.[1]
AD 41:	Gaius Caesar is assassinated by officers of the Praetorian Guard at the age of 29 and is succeeded by Tiberius **Claudius** Drusus.
AD 43:	Four legions invade Britain under the command of Aulus Plautius. Claudius briefly visits the new province.

[1] *Decline and Fall: Were the Romans Poisoned?* Peter Cooper, FPS, The Pharmaceutical Journal, December 22 and 29, 1973.

AD 54:	Claudius dies, probably poisoned by his second wife, Agrippina the Younger, who secures the succession for her son **Nero** Claudius Caesar Drusus Germanicus, who assassinates her in AD 59.
AD 60:	The Druids and other anti-Roman elements on Mona Insulis (Anglesey) are massacred by Suetonius Paulinus; this operation is followed immediately by a serious revolt in south-east Britain, led by the implacable Icenian Queen Boudica.
AD 61:	Paulinus crushes the Boudican Revolt.
AD 64:	A large area of the city of Rome is destroyed by fire. The Christian sect is blamed initially, but the Emperor himself is suspected latterly of deliberately firing the city to make way for the construction of his Golden House.
AD 66:	A major revolt breaks out in Judaea; Vespasianus is sent to restore order.
AD 68:	Julius Vindex, Governor of Central Gaul revolts against Nero, but is killed at the battle of Vesontio (Besançon). The aging Sulpicius **Galba**, Governor of Nearer Spain, revolts also and is supported by the Senate. He marches on Rome, and Nero commits suicide.
AD 69:	The Year of the Three Caesars. Galba becomes unpopular and earns the particular displeasure of Marcus Salvius **Otho** by not choosing him as his successor. Otho arranges Galba's murder and succeeds with the support of a large number of legions. However, Aulus **Vitellius** is hailed Emperor by the Rhine legions and marches on Rome. He defeats Otho at the first battle of Bedriacum, near Cremona, and Otho commits suicide. Vitellius succeeds, only to learn that the eastern legions have declared for their general Vespasianus. The forces of Vitellius are defeated by the pro-Vespasianus general Primus at the second battle of Bedriacum. Flavius Sabinus **Vespasianus** succeeds and the civil war closes.

FVNDATORIQVIETIS

A section of the triumphal relief from Trajan's Forum, later incorporated into the Arch of Constantine. The sculpture shows cavalry wearing mail and scale body defences, and legionary infantry wearing cuirasses with laminations on the breast instead of breast-plates. (Trajan's Column, Rome)

AD 70: The city of Jerusalem falls to the besieging Roman force under the command of Vespasianus' son Titus. General Flavius Silva is sent to invest the Herodian fortress of Masada, which has been occupied by a band of Sicarii and others of the anti-Roman faction.

AD 73: Masada falls. The besieged Jews commit suicide rather than surrender to the Romans.

AD 79: Vespasianus dies after a stable reign and is succeeded by his son **Titus**.

AD 81: Titus dies prematurely at the age of 42, having completed the building of the great Flavian amphitheatre at Rome, known today as the Colosseum, begun by his father in AD 72. Titus is succeeded by his younger brother, Titus Flavius **Domitianus**. (Rumours that Domitianus was responsible for Titus' early death were never proven; however, Domitianus was an unpleasant character and was doubtless bitterly jealous of his popular brother.)

AD 89: Antonius Saturninus, Governor of Upper Germany, revolts against Domitianus, but is brought to battle and defeated on the plain of Andernach by Maximus, the Governor of Lower Germany.

AD 96: Domitianus is finally murdered, bringing the Flavian Dynasty to an end. He is succeeded by Marcus Cocceius **Nerva**.

AD 98: Nerva dies having adopted the 44-year-old Governor of Upper Germany, Marcus Ulpius **Trajanus**, as his successor—a most fortunate choice. Trajanus proves to be an excellent soldier and a statesman, a rare combination. Considered to be the finest Roman Emperor, he extends the Empire to its largest geographical size.

INTRODUCTION

'Had previous chroniclers neglected to speak in praise of History in general, it might perhaps have been necessary for me to recommend everyone to choose for study and welcome such treatises as the present, since man has no more ready corrective of conduct than knowledge of the past. . . For who is so worthless or indolent as not to wish to know by what means and under what system of polity the Romans in less than 53 years have succeeded in subjecting nearly the whole inhabited world to their sole government, a thing unique in history?' (Polybius)

Probably the most fruitful of the Romans for such study are their soldiers—men of great courage, determination and ability, whose faces still stare silently out at us with an air of grave dignity from sculptures once bright with paint and bronze ornament.

Though the common soldiers have left no known written account of their experiences, the earth has yielded large quantities of objects in varying states of preservation, which have enabled modern man to learn much of the life of the ancient soldier. Literature, too, has survived from antiquity, providing us with valuable clues and even direct and accurate descriptions of military equipment, which are increasingly being verified by archaeological finds.

Quite detailed information has also been derived from sculptural works, the foremost of these being the great column erected in the early second century AD by the Emperor Marcus Ulpius Trajanus to commemorate his victories over the Dacians. We can still see, spiralling up this 132-foot monument, the army of Trajan performing the various deeds of the campaign and going about their multitude of military tasks. This has, of course, proved to be of inestimable value to historians not only from the aspect of military equipment, but also

with regard to the appearance of forts and bridges of a more temporary nature of which little or nothing survives. The partial reconstruction of a turf and timber rampart and gate in its original position at the Lunt Fort, Baginton, near Coventry is largely based upon information derived from this monument.

While Trajan's Column (a two-part cast of which may be seen in the Victoria and Albert Museum, London) has proved to contain some surprisingly accurate details of Roman military practice, it must still be treated with a great deal of caution, especially with regard to the proportions of certain objects such as shields; these are invariably shown on a reduced scale. A similar concession was made to aesthetics by narrowing the cheek-guards of helmets in order that the faces of the men would become more visible. This vast work, which was no doubt painted originally, like so many other ancient sculptures, would also have bristled with bronze weapons where now there are only empty hands; the bronze has long since vanished into the crucibles of later ages.

ARMY COMPOSITION

The Roman military of this period may be divided into two distinct parts, the legions and the auxilia, with a marked social division between them.

The ranks of a legion were entirely filled by Roman citizens. This does not mean that they were all men of Italian origin, but that the individual, be he a Gaul, Iberian, or whatever, possessed the coveted 'citizenship', which was hereditary—for example, it will be recalled that the father of Saul of Tarsus was granted the citizenship for services to the Roman army in the capacity of tentmaker. This would have meant that, had he possessed the required mental and physical development, the young Saul would have been eligible for service with a legion. As we know, he did make use of one of

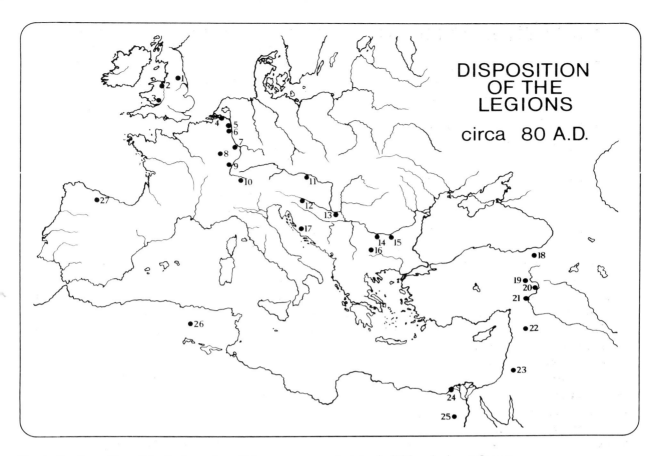

DISPOSITION
OF THE
LEGIONS
circa 80 A.D.

Key to the disposition of the Legions AD 80:
(1) Legio IX Hispana at York.
(2) Legiones XX Valeria and II Adiutrix at Chester.
(3) Legio II Augusta at Caerleon.
(4) Legiones XXII Primigenia and X Gemina at Nijmegen.
(5) Legio VI Victrix at Neuss.
(6) Legio XXI Rapax at Bonn.
(7) Legio XIV Gemina at Mainz.
(8) Legio I Adiutrix at or near Mainz.
(9) Legio VIII Augusta at Strasbourg.
(10) Legio XI Claudia at Windisch.
(11) Legio XV Apollinaris at Carnuntum.
(12) Legio XIII Gemina at Poetovio.
(13) Legio VII Claudia at Viminiacum.
(14) Legio V Macedonica at Oescus.
(15) Legio I Italica at Novae.
(16) Legio V Alaudae on or near the Danube.
(17) Legio IV Flavia Firma at Burnum.
(18) Legio XVI Flavia Firma at Satala.
(19) Legio XII Fulminata at Melitene.
(20) Legio VI Ferrata at Samosata.
(21) Legio IV Sythica at Cyrrhus.
(22) Legio III Gallica at Danabe near Damascus.
(23) Legio X Fretensis at Jerusalem.
(24) Legio XXII Deiotariana at Alexandria.
(25) Legio III Cyrenaica at Coptos near Luxor.
(26) Legio III Augusta at Ammaedara near Tebessa.
(27) Legio VII Gemina at Leon.

the rights bestowed by his citizenship, in that he made legal appeal to the very head of the Roman State, the Emperor himself.

A large number of the legionary soldiers were skilled tradesmen. Skills which would be acquired during the early years of their service enabled the men to increase their rates of pay and to be promoted to the rank of *immunis*. No doubt this rank excused them from such necessary but irksome tasks as latrine duty. The presence of these skilled men within the ranks rendered a legion, as far as possible, a self-sufficient unit, which could provide its own forts and fortifications and other structures, such as

bridges and war machinery. Since the men were being trained almost wholly as military engineers and professional killers, it is hardly surprising that one seldom encounters a well-lettered inscription or artistic relief that was the product of their hands. Such things require a great deal of aptitude and experience, and when accomplished works of the kind are found in a military context they are more likely to be the efforts of civilians employed specifically for such purposes.

The legions were supported by the non-citizen *auxilia*, which in Caesar's time was not a regular arm of the Roman forces and therefore did not

A section of a relief at Rome showing Praetorian guards carrying javelins with lead (or possibly cast bronze) loads, and long shields of the late Republic, which had become a traditional part of their equipment by the 1st century AD when this relief was carved. (The Cancelleria Relief, in the collection of the Vatican Museum)

conform to standard Roman unit strengths. Under Augustus, auxiliary units were integrated into the Roman army on a permanent basis, with a fixed annual recruitment, and organised after the Roman manner in three types of unit (see diagram). The infantry cohorts were named after either their tribal or national origin. The cavalry, on the other hand, were often identified by the name of the commanding officer in the early days, those titles remaining part of the unit's identification even though the man concerned was long dead: e.g. *Ala Augusta Gallorum* Petriana *Milliaria Civium Romanorum*—after Titus Pomponius Petra, whose name was to be found a century later when his old unit was serving on Hadrian's Wall at Carlisle.

The third type of auxiliary unit, the *Cohors Equitata*, was regarded as inferior to the other two, and this was clearly reflected in their equipment. Evidently this inferior status did not detract from the valour of the soldiers in one case at least, for a

surviving bronze diploma refers to the honourable discharge before expiration of service of an entire *Cohors Equitata*—the *Ulpia Torquata*, which was raised in Britain and had distinguished itself in the Dacian Wars under Trajan.

To obtain such a diploma was the ambition of every auxiliary—horse and foot alike—for it meant that the citizenship of Rome, probably the main inducement to enlist, was now theirs, and they were free to return home. Honourable discharge was normally achieved by serving out the agreed time period, some 25 years; and now that the auxiliary soldier was a citizen he would enjoy privileges under Roman law which also improved his family's prospects within the Roman system.

It appears that the Romans even took care over the morale of their auxiliaries, at least in the early days of the Empire, by posting the units fairly close to their place of origin, presumably in order to prevent feelings of disquiet among the troops at being cut off from familiar surroundings. Later, as necessity dictated, such niceties were overlooked and units were posted far afield, which occasioned at least two mutinies.

Naturally enough, the legionaries regarded the non-citizens of the *auxilia* as inferiors; but it was the auxiliaries who really manned the frontiers of the Empire and policed the Provinces, and it was they who fought and won the final battle of the invasion of Britain. Their contribution to the establishment of the Roman World may perhaps have been rather badly underestimated in favour of the 'esprit de corps' of the legions.

At the time of Vespasian some of the existing auxiliary units were enlarged and new units of greater strength were raised. These consisted of ten-century infantry cohorts, 24-troop cavalry regiments, and a ten-century cohort with eight cavalry troops as a larger form of *Cohors Equitata*. These new units were called *Milliaria* or 'thousand strong', but in fact contained rather fewer men. The smaller auxiliary units were called *Quingenaria* or 'five hundred strong', again being slightly weaker in practice than the title suggests.

As generations came and went, the sons of time-expired auxiliaries, now of citizen status, joined the same locally-based units with which their fathers had served; the rigid distinction between the legions and the *auxilia* began to fade, though it did not finally disappear until the reign of the Emperor Caracalla in AD 212.

ENTRY, TRAINING AND CAMPAIGN ROUTINES

Enrolment under normal circumstances, that is to say in time of comparable peace, was a rather similar process to that in use in some armies today. The applicant was ordered to appear before a board of examining officers, men experienced in the selection of the most suitable fighting material. The ideal was a man six *pes* tall (about five feet ten inches), of good eyesight and a strong, well-proportioned physique, a man of generally good bearing. After passing the board the young man, usually about 18 years old, began a period called *probatio*, during which he underwent a more stringent medical examination. His character would also be closely scrutinised during this period, and he would no doubt be asked many questions;

lazy men, thieves and the extremely immoral were not welcome in the Roman army, and when serious lapses did occur, such as a man being caught asleep on sentry duty, they were dealt with very severely indeed, often with fatal results.

Once accepted for service, recruits swore an oath of allegiance to the Emperor, probably before the Eagle of his legion, and was then posted to a special training camp, several examples of which have been identified in Britain. There the raw men were taught to dig ditches, build ramparts and look after their equipment, part of which they had to purchase out of their pay—usually the items which they would have had to buy in civil life as a matter of course.

Inescapably, a large part of the training was devoted to 'square-bashing' and route-marching with full equipment; learning how to adjust correctly the great legionary shield on a baldric, and how to carry the kit-pole in the left hand. As in any age, the recruits were no doubt awkward at first, but found these skills second nature by the time basic training was over.

The Romans exercised great care over rigidity of formation, since this was believed to be the key to safety on the march and success in battle. The legionaries were taught two paces, a short clipped step called, by the Roman historian Vegetius, the

A section of the relief of Trajan's Column showing legionaries building defences and setting up a ballista, while auxiliaries engage a force of Dacians. (Trajan's Column, Rome)

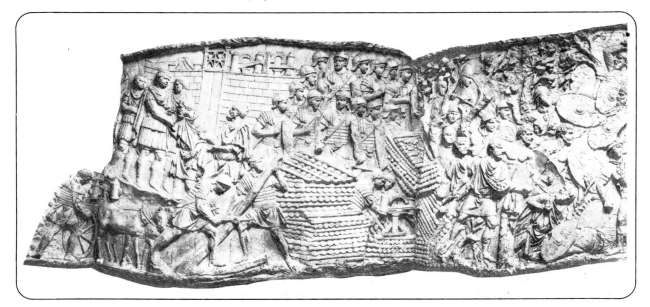

Mailed legionaries from the Aemilius Paulus victory monument at Delphi, erected to commemorate the Roman victory over King Perseus of Macedonia at Pydna in 168 BC. The shields are virtually identical to a surviving specimen from Egypt, which had a wooden boss covering the horizontal handgrip.

The thorax was avoided, most probably because that part of the torso has a superior natural defence and is not so easily pierced as the boneless abdomen. Cutting strokes were avoided as much as possible, though an enemy unhelmeted was clearly too tempting a target for a swift downward blow on the skull to be missed (as witness skeletal finds at Maiden Castle). However, such a stroke necessarily exposed the entire right side: better to keep the arm low and avoid the risk of a possible 'sucking wound' in the rib-cage, leading to lung collapse. The Romans were said to have despised enemies who laid about themselves with long slashing blades, and despatched them with ease.

The recruits would also be taught to use the legionary shield as a weapon as much as a defence. The boss of the shield was certainly used to punch opponents and the edge may also have been used to strike an enemy in the face; the latter method is shown in early gladiatorial sculpture, but might have required rather more strength to achieve than was possessed by the average soldier. Either method would doubtless have the effect of causing the enemy to raise his arms to steady himself, thereby exposing his abdomen to a quick stab from the Roman's sword to end the matter.

Whether or not the javelin had to be delivered with a high degree of accuracy is questionable: the Emperor Hadrian, reviewing troops, praised the accuracy of their throwing, but launching those dreadful weapons at a packed enemy force was bound to do fearful harm wherever these long iron heads struck. Caesar tells us that the javelin was capable of piercing the enemies' shields and pinning them together, proving to be so troublesome to

'military pace', doubtless employed when tight drill was required; and the 'full pace', a longer, easier gait, used on the march for long periods. Precisely how the Romans taught their men accurate marching steps is not known, but one guesses at something akin to a modern pace-stick. In any event, the Romans do not appear to have had drumbeats as an aid to the step, either in training or subsequently; in fact the drum seems to have been unknown in the Roman army.

On the march, the soldiers were expected to cover a distance of 20 Roman miles at the 'military pace' in five hours; when the 'full pace' was used, a distance of 24 miles was achieved in the same period of time. Taking the Roman mile as being 1,620 yards, the full pace is a rate of nearly four-and-a-half miles per hour: a good measure by most standards, this must surely have applied to troop movements on good roads, for it would have been quite impossible to have accomplished these distances over rough and probably hostile terrain.

No less important, of course, would be weapon training, particularly the correct use of the short sword. Recruits were encouraged to attack six-foot wooden stakes fixed into the ground, using dummy shields and swords. The Romans used their swords to stab, keeping the hilt low and thrusting at the face, abdominal cavity and legs of an opponent.

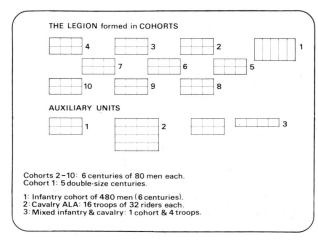

THE LEGION formed in COHORTS

AUXILIARY UNITS

Cohorts 2–10: 6 centuries of 80 men each.
Cohort 1: 5 double-size centuries.

1: Infantry cohort of 480 men (6 centuries).
2: Cavalry ALA: 16 troops of 32 riders each.
3: Mixed infantry & cavalry: 1 cohort & 4 troops.

A bronze boss from a *clipeus* or flat oval shield. Elaborately decorated with engraving and punching, it was most probably a cavalry piece used for the *hippika gymnasia* or cavalry sports.

The intricately decorated *scutum* boss which belonged to a legionary—Junius Dubitatus—who served with Legio VIII Augusta, presumably after AD 70 when that legion was stationed on the upper Rhine. Since the legion is not recorded as having been stationed in Britain, this find from the River Tyne on the north British frontier probably indicates the presence of a 'vexillation' or detachment only. (In the collection of the British Museum)

extricate that they preferred to drop the encumbered shields and face the legionaries unprotected. The extreme difficulty in removing the javelins probably describes the effect of a type of javelin head which had a small barbed tip, used in Caesar's time; an example was recovered from the site of the siege of Alesia, undertaken by Caesar during his conquest of Gaul.

The march and the marching camp

The legionaries illustrated as A3 and E2 in the colour plates show equipment slung for the march in friendly territory; this may be assumed from the position of the helmets, which would be worn on the march when hostilities were at all likely. Legionaries portrayed on Trajan's Column are shown to carry a pole in the left hand, apparently to support the soldiers' personal effects and mess equipment. This consisted of a bag which probably contained a military cloak or *sagum*, which may have doubled as a blanket; bathing and shaving tackle; spare thongs; equipment for scouring and polishing his armour and weapons; and doubtless his most prized possessions such as his decorations—such objects would not have been entrusted to the baggage train. Below the kit-bag may be seen the mess equipment: a mess tin or *patera*; a camp kettle; and a sack with a cord net protector, which probably held rations of grain, bacon, cheese or any of the other extraordinary foods that may have been gathered by forage, said to have been eaten by Roman soldiers. A reinforced leather satchel is also shown on the Column, and this probably contained the soldier's tools for construction work. The remainder of the equipment belonging to each eight-man section (*contubernium*) was carried on a mule allotted to the section.

The order of march used by the legions as they advanced into Galilee during the Jewish uprising of AD 66–73 is given by the Jewish historian Joseph ben Matthias, better known as Flavius Josephus, in his extremely vivid and apparently accurate account of the insurrection—*The Jewish War*. Josephus refers to it as the 'usual' Roman marching order; however, one might expect a great deal to have depended upon the prevailing situation and the discretion of the army commander.

The vanguard was formed of light-armed auxiliaries and bowmen. These were to engage and

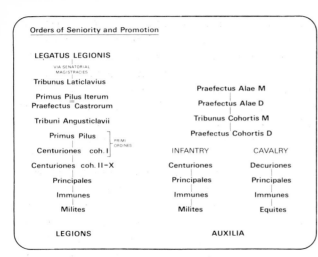

Orders of Seniority and Promotion

LEGATUS LEGIONIS
│ *VIA SENATORIAL MAGISTRACIES*

Tribunus Laticlavius

Primus Pilus Iterum
Praefectus Castrorum

Tribuni Angusticlavii

Primus Pilus — *PRIMI ORDINES*

Centuriones coh. I

Centuriones coh. II–X

Principales

Immunes

Milites

LEGIONS

Praefectus Alae M

Praefectus Alae D

Tribunus Cohortis M

Praefectus Cohortis D

INFANTRY	CAVALRY
Centuriones	Decuriones
Principales	Principales
Immunes	Immunes
Milites	Equites

AUXILIA

repel skirmishers and to probe likely ambush cover. The head of the column proper was a body of heavily armed Roman troops, mounted and on foot. Next were the surveyors, drawn from the centuries of the legions, carrying the instruments for marking out a camp. Behind them came the pioneers (*antecursores*), probably carrying *dolabrae* for tree-felling and other tools. These men cleared the path of the army so that the already burdened soldiers would not be troubled further by difficult terrain. A strong cavalry force followed with the commander's baggage and that of his staff, behind which rode the commander himself, surrounded by the finest of his infantry and cavalry and a body of pikemen (*hastati*). Then came the legionary cavalry; Josephus indicates that there were 120 of these permanently attached to a legion, probably employed as scouts and messengers. These horsemen were followed by the 'artillery', consisting of *catapultae*, *ballistae*, rams and other war machinery carried in parts on mules. Behind these came the generals, cohort commanders and tribunes with their infantry guard marching before the sacred *aquila*, which was surrounded by the other legion standards and followed by the trumpeters with their instruments. The main column of infantry stretched out behind, marching six abreast in close dressing, with centurions watching the discipline of the formation. Next came the baggage-train with the tents and general construction implements, supervised by the camp 'servants'. The rear of the column was comprised of mercenaries, with a strong rearguard of infantry and cavalry whom one might believe were placed there as much to prevent the

mercenaries making off in the event of a serious assault being made against them, as to perform the normal duties of that office.

When the required distance had been covered, the surveyors (and presumably the pioneers) were sent forward to mark out a chosen site for the night camp. More conscientious commanders preferred to select the site in person. The size and construction of these 'marching camps' was laid down in manuals and they were like a playing-card in plan. From the remains of such camps it is evident that the plan was varied to suit the terrain, but mainly they adhere to the rectangular shape with rounded corners. The size of the camp was determined by a formula: 200 times the square root of the number of cohorts to be accommodated giving the short sides, one and one-half times that for the long sides.

The surveyors put up four big flags where the corners of the camp were to be and then marked off the positions of the four gates, one in each side. The two in the short sides were named *porta praetoria* and *porta decumana*. Those in the remaining sides were *porta principalis sinistra* and *porta principalis dextra*—left and right respectively from the main gate, the *porta praetoria*. The street plan of the camp was basically a cross, the *via praetoria* running between the main and rear gates and the *via principalis* between the side gates.

Assuming the site had been cleared and prepared by the pioneers and surveyors, the main body of the army now marched straight into the place without a halt, and dumped off kit in the areas allotted to each section; every man knew his own position, so all was accomplished without noise or delay. Men were detailed to throw up the enclosing rampart, which was usually quite shallow, little more than a yard wide and deep in the ditch, with the spoil thrown back to the camp side to form the rampart. *Pila muralia* or rampart stakes were then forced into the top of the bank and lashed together to form a palisade. These wooden stakes were about five feet in length, pointed at both ends and slightened in the middle to take the lashing.

While engaged in building such ramparts, the legionaries stacked their arms close at hand. The stack was made by ramming the shoe of the javelin into the ground and leaning the shield against it; the helmet was then tied to the shaft of the javelin and allowed to fall over the face of the shield, thus preventing the latter from being blown over. This method of stacking may be seen in several instances on Trajan's Column. The soldiers were required to wear their sidearms during construction of this nature, probably when the enemy was in the vicinity; one man is known to have been executed for not doing so, but this was probably an object lesson, since the event occurred during a known period of restoration of discipline.

Other men were posted as sentries, while the remainder set about erecting the sturdy leather tents in orderly lines with avenues between them. Their appearance was not unlike some modern ridge tents, with low verticals at the sides, and end-flaps. The main part of the tent was made from squares of goat hide, and sculptural representations of this feature gave rise to the misconception that Roman tents were provided with a rope net of large mesh. The tent covered an area of ten Roman feet square; the Roman foot or *pes* is equivalent to 0.962 foot Imperial measure.

Excavations of the Roman siege camps at the Herodian fortress of Masada have revealed that the tents were placed over recesses with side 'benches' dug into the ground, providing more standing room inside the tents; but it seems unlikely that tents would be 'dug in' like this for a night's marching camp, and this feature was probably more typical of camps which were to be inhabited for a considerable length of time.

words concerning the origin of the leather 'armour' so often used, and its lack of defensive quality.

This misconception arose very largely from the apparently common Roman habit of painting on to their sculptures parts which were tedious to portray with a chisel. They may also have reproduced the appearance of mail by making indentations into soft gesso with a curved tool. By the time the artists of the Renaissance began to portray the classical warrior, most or all of the painted or plastered parts had weathered away, leaving the mail shirts looking smooth and very like leather jerkins. Perhaps if the artists had taken the trouble to look closely at the representations of auxiliaries on Trajan's Column, they would have observed that the 'jerkins' were in fact worked with close-set vertical zigzag lines, clearly intended to represent the texture of mail.

If one examines leather as a defensive material and then tries to reconcile its properties with the forms of body defence used by the Romans, it becomes perfectly apparent that it would have been quite useless: either it would not have been proof against the weapons of the ancient world, or if it *had* been thick and hard enough to withstand a spear thrust or sword cut, the wearer would have experienced extreme difficulty in performing any normal movements, let alone the violent motions required in an action.

Plan of the common *caliga* **laid out flat. These boots were provided with soles approximately ½in thick and heavily studded with domed hobnails of iron.**

ARMS AND ARMOUR

Body Defences

In view of the understandable limitations of theatrical and film costume departments, they are obliged for one reason or another to persist in arming their Roman soldiers with defences constructed from leather; and since this image appears to impress itself upon unwitting audiences, it might not be unwise to include in this work a few

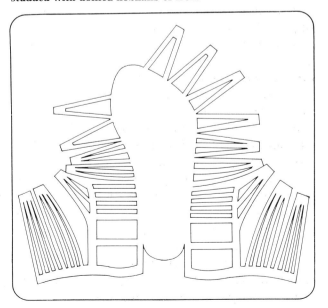

Leather did feature to some extent in this period, but only as *pteruges*, the series of hide strips appended to corselets of mail, scale or plate armour. No doubt the hide used for *pteruges* would have been somewhat akin to the 'buff leather' so familiar in portrayals of soldiers of the 17th century—though since the latter type requires an extract from the sperm whale for its manufacture, the similarity would be slight. It is interesting, however, to note how little faith was actually placed in the buff coats, as evidenced by the addition of an iron cuirass and a bridle or elbow gauntlet on the left forearm.

To return to the Romans, the addition of *pteruges*

The auxiliary shield from Doncaster, thought to have belonged to the garrison of Danum in the second half of the 1st century AD. An example of auxiliary troops continuing to carry native equipment. Rectangular shields were uncommon among auxiliaries, but may be seen occasionally in sculpture.

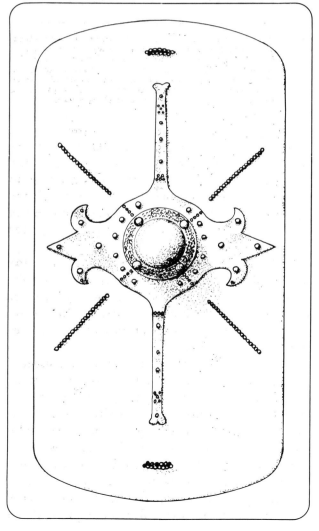

would have meant a valuable saving in mail manufacture, and it seems that to that end they were prepared to sacrifice some of the highly effective protection afforded to the upper arm and thigh.

Precisely which nation was responsible for the invention of mail, called *hamata* by the Romans, remains a matter for debate. The earliest examples of mail are quoted as having been found in Scythian tombs of the 5th century BC; however, it seems most unlikely that people such as the Scythians, who enjoyed a nomadic way of life, would have been able to develop the quite advanced tooling required for successful mail manufacture. The next indication of the use of mail is a painting of a mercenary soldier from Galatia (modern Turkey, but an area apparently settled in early times by Celtic peoples) wearing a short, sleeveless hauberk, dated to the 3rd or 2nd century BC. The Roman writer Varro states that the Romans acquired their knowledge of mail-making from the Celtic Gauls, and it was considered that they were its inventors. Whilst there is no evidence to prove or disprove Varro on this point, the Celts were an inventive people with a superb mastery of metal working, perfectly able to achieve such an innovation. But exactly the same can equally well be said of the peoples of the Middle East—the Assyrians made beautiful iron helmets as early as the 8th to 7th centuries BC (see British Museum) and therefore the required technology could very possibly have been developed in that region.

Whether mail originated in western Europe or in the Middle East, in view of the Scythian finds its date of origin must surely be as early as the 6th century BC; and its continued use by the Romans is evidenced initially by the Aemilius Paulus victory monument at Delphi, dated to the first half of the 2nd century BC, and the altar of Domitius Ahenobarbus, dated to the second half of the 1st century BC. Both these sculptures depict legionaries wearing mail defences, the essential difference between them being that those of the latter appear to have been slightly lengthened in the main body of the hauberks.

The Romans appear to have inherited two types of shoulder doublings: one was cut in a fashion reminiscent of Greek linen cuirasses, and the second in a form of cape, more probably of Celtic origin, which did not require leathering in its early form (though the Romans appear to have used leathers to back both types by the 1st century AD). This was clearly necessary in the case of the Greek type, which collapses into long, narrow strips when unleathered, and is totally unworkable.

As a defence, mail has two very considerable drawbacks: it is extremely laborious to make, and while it affords complete freedom of movement to the wearer, it is very heavy. The manufacturing difficulty was partly overcome by the use of alternate rows of stamped rings which did not require to be joined. These must have been a blessing to the ancient mail-maker, and it would be most interesting to know what kind of tools they used to make them. The stamped rings still had to be linked together with riveted wire rings, but the time involved in making a complete hauberk must have been cut by as much as a quarter. A less costly form of mail, probably Celtic, employed stamped rings in the same manner, but the wire rings were simply cut from the coil and left as a butted circlet, without riveting.

The weight of the mail, when unbelted, fell entirely onto the wearer's shoulders, and with a hauberk which weighed perhaps as much as 15lbs this would be very tiring and more than a little uncomfortable. This was countered by the military belt drawn tightly about the waist, thereby causing part of the weight to be distributed onto the hips; the use of *pteruges* could also reduce the drag of the mail.

The use by the Romans of scale shirts (*loricae squamatae*), judging by their sculptures, does not appear to have been as extensive as mail, with the possible exception of the cavalry, and the infantry officer class, including the *principales*. This is hardly surprising, since as a defence, scale was far inferior to mail, being neither as strong nor as flexible. The scales were never thick enough to withstand a good cut and remain undamaged; and the hauberk could be pierced with relative ease by an upthrust of sword or spear, which would have made it rather an unsatisfactory defence for a cavalry trooper engaging footsoldiers armed with spears.

The method of manufacture was to overlap the scales and fasten them together in horizontal rows by means of loose, rough rings passed through small holes in the sides of the scales. The rows were then

The cavalry 'sports' helmet from Ribchester in Lancashire. The mask was hinged at the top and tied down with a strap and buckle round the nape. The helmet is of bronze and had a silvered face. It was fitted with a crest, most probably of horse-hair, and streamers, perhaps of the same material, tied to rings at the sides of the skull. This very fine example of the armourer's art may be seen in the British Museum.

applied to the foundation of rough linen (or occasionally, thin hide) by laying a strand of yarn along the face of the scales over the larger holes in the upper edges and then stitching through the holes and round the yarn. This had the effect of minimising the metal's tendency to fray the stitching-thread.

Scale did have its advantages: it could be made by virtually anyone, and was very simple to repair. Cost, just as much of a problem to the ancients as it is today, was doubtless a consideration—scale armour of the more common types was cheap in comparison with mail.

It was probably early in the reign of the Emperor Tiberius that the first type of laminated iron cuirass (*lorica segmentata*) made its appearance, perhaps as a result of the enormous loss of equipment that was suffered by the Rhine legions in AD 9. The replacement of all the lost material must have presented a considerable problem, for mail shirts are very time consuming in manufacture. The iron plate *segmentata*, by contrast, could be made with the equipment available to the Romans in probably no more than 60 hours, given the sheet iron.

These remarkably flexible armours were probably the first iron plate defences ever devised, and may have been partially developed from gladiatorial equipment. Whether or not they were a purely Roman invention is not certain; however, there is no evidence to suggest otherwise. The idea of using lames in the construction of simple arm-guards was known to the Greeks, but it is a very

The pierced, engraved and silvered locket of a 'Pompeii' pattern sword scabbard. The two figures are representations of the war-god Mars. The piece probably had palmettes at the lower corners.

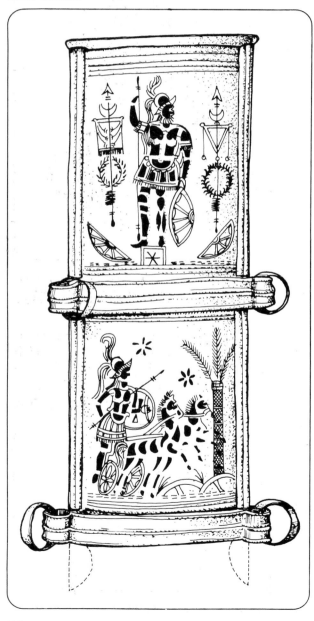

considerable step to the production of entire cuirasses.

It is certain that the cuirass now classified as Corbridge 'A' was quite widely issued by the time the Emperor Claudius ordered the invasion of Britain in AD 43, and the recent discovery of an unused shoulder-splint plate conforming very closely to the type 'B' cuirass, found on the site of the invasion supply base of Legio II Augusta at Chichester, suggests that the second of the Corbridge cuirass types was already in circulation by that date.

While hundreds of fragments from cuirasses of this type have been found on sites where legionaries have been present, and reconstructions attempted, it is only as a result of excavations in 1964 on the site of the Roman station of Corstopitum (Corbridge) near Hadrian's Wall that the true appearance and construction of these armours has become established. Buried beneath the floor of one of the Roman buildings, the remains of an iron-bound chest was discovered, containing, among other items, bundles of completely oxidised iron armour. From these have emerged the two patterns of cuirass of 1st century date known as Corbridge 'A' and 'B'; the major difference between them is the method used to fasten the girdle unit to the collar sections (see colour plates E2 and E3).

The laminated cuirasses were obviously superior to mail with regard to ease of manufacture and preservation, but most particularly in view of their weight, which was as little as 12lbs, depending upon the thickness of plate used. Inevitably, they had some disadvantages as well, notably the loss of protection to the thighs and upper arms. Quality control in manufacture also provided something of a problem; weak or badly made fittings, which frequently broke, must have given the legionary armourers a continual round of repairs, and it was not until the later years of the 1st century that a new type of cuirass was developed which was devoid of almost all fittings which would break easily and were not really necessary. This type of cuirass, which we call the 'Newstead' (see colour plate F3), after fragments found on the site of the fort of Trimontium (Newstead) near Melrose, Scotland, was strong and perfectly functional. It is this pattern which is to be seen in the majority of the representations on Trajan's Column.

What is most probably a fourth type of cuirass, similar to the Newstead, is shown in various sculptures and small figurines. This pattern, actual remains of which have yet to be discovered, is clearly depicted on a section of the frieze from Trajan's Forum (see photographic plate), which was subsequently re-used in the construction of the Arch of Constantine. Instead of the single-piece breast-plates of the Newstead pattern, this type apparently was fitted with continuous laminations all the way up to the neck, in much the same way as the upper back-plates of the Corbridge cuirasses had been.

Helmets

The head-pieces worn by Caesar's legionaries were more often of the rather simple and not very well finished Montefortino type 'C' shown in colour plate A1. Such helmets were clearly mass-produced, probably as a result of the Marian reforms which had permitted enlistment in the legions by large numbers of poor men, who could not afford to purchase costly armour, as had been the custom previously. These helmets were crested with a brush and tail of horse-hair mounted on a single pin, which was inserted into a drill-hole in the knob on the top of the helmet crown. Helmets of this type continued in service during the 1st century AD.

During the reign of the Emperor Augustus the first of the 'Coolus' helmets appeared in the Roman army. These had a more natural skull shape to the bowl and a larger neck-guard than the Montefortino pattern. The skull form was of Gallic origin, the earliest specimen having been found in the Marne

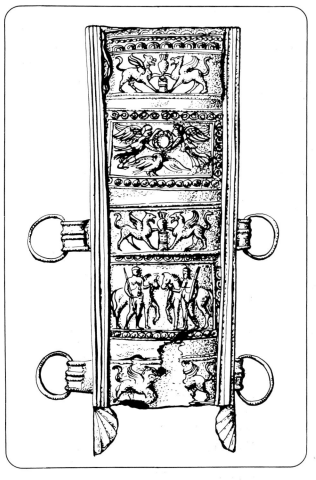

The locket from a cavalry sword scabbard. The stamped decoration on the face is applied thin bronze sheet, and the style of decoration suggests a cavalry unit of Thracian origin.

Basin. The Roman version was somewhat improved by the addition of a frontal reinforce or 'peak' which prevented blows from striking the forepart of the skull. The early Roman Coolus helmets of type 'C' had no crest fastenings, unlike almost all of their

A leather tent—*papilio*—reconstructed from goat hide fragments found at Newstead in Scotland by the late Sir Ian Richmond. The tent housed an eight-man section called a *contubernium*.

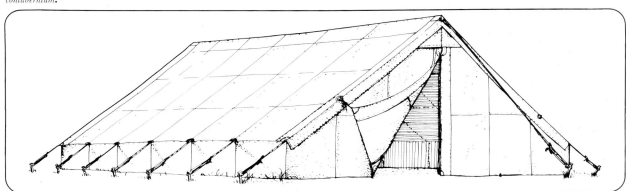

cousins. Coolus type 'E', shown in figure A3, is based on the well-known Walbrook helmet, which may be seen in the British Museum; this helmet not only had a spike for the attachment of a central horse-hair crest, but thin bronze tubes soldered to the sides of the skull for the mounting of plumes (see

author's reconstruction of a Coolus 'E' helmet). Cresting practices may have varied from legion to legion, according to its area of origin, or its status, or possibly there may be some significance of rank for which the evidence is currently obscure.

The first half of the 1st century AD saw a very much larger neck-guard develop, culminating in the Haguenau helmet—Coolus type 'G'—in the third quarter of the century. The Haguenau specimen has a flat, almost semi-circular neck-

Four views of an Imperial Italic type 'C' bronze helmet from the River Po, probably lost during the civil war of AD 68–69, which began with the suicide of Nero and ended with the establishment of the Flavian dynasty. (In the collection of the Museo Stibbert, Florence)

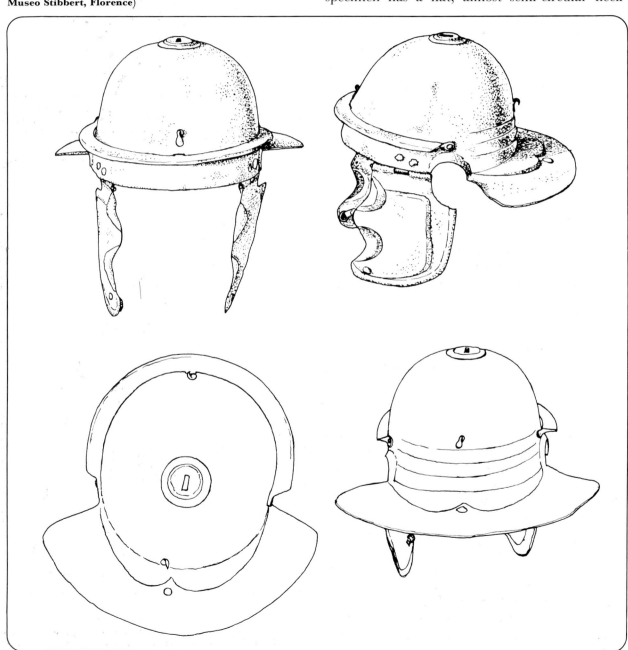

guard and a bulbous skull of considerable height, with a crest spike and side-tubes for plumes. At about the same time a new pattern of bronze helmet was being made, probably in Italy, of which two specimens survive (see author's drawings of the Imperial Italic type 'C' helmet from the River Po at Cremona). Both of these helmets contain Gallic features which are common to the iron helmets of this date, but have no eyebrows and are fitted with crest fastenings of Italian type (see colour plate C1).

The production of iron helmets had been practiced in Gaul prior to the subjugation by Caesar in the mid-1st century BC, and once the Gauls were incorporated into the Roman sphere the iron helmet began to appear in the ranks of the legions. Colour plate E shows three types of iron helmet that had been evolved by the middle years of the 1st century AD, denoted Imperial Gallic types 'F' and 'E'. The helmets of Gallic origin were usually of a superior finish to those produced by the factories of Italy at that time—probably because iron working is very much more difficult than bronze, and the technology was new to the Italian armourers.

The iron helmets were frequently decorated with small stamped bosses, sometimes with fine ribbing and red enamelled centres—a typically Celtic feature. The peaks were occasionally provided with a fine strip of reeded bronze along the forward edge, but one is inclined to feel that such intricacies would not have survived for more than a matter of minutes in action. Oddly enough, none of the surviving helmets bear marks which can be attributed with any certainty to combat damage. The helmet of Italic type 'D' from the River Rhine at Mainz displays a series of nicks along the forward edge of the peak which were thought to be the results of an action; however, the marks in question are placed at very regular intervals, which can only mean that they were introduced deliberately, most probably in modern times.

The manufacture of iron helmets did not preclude the continued supply of bronze head-pieces, as may be seen by the author's reconstruction of the Mainz bronze legionary helmet, also illustrated in colour plate F1, which was made during the mid-second half of the 1st century AD. No doubt the continued manufacture of bronze pieces was partly caused by the very slow trickle of iron

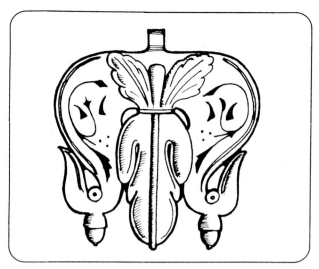

Cast bronze cavalry harness pendant, silvered and inlaid with black niello. These pendants were normally suspended below a *phalera* or decorated disc by means of the pierced lug at the top. (After Dr. Graham Webster)

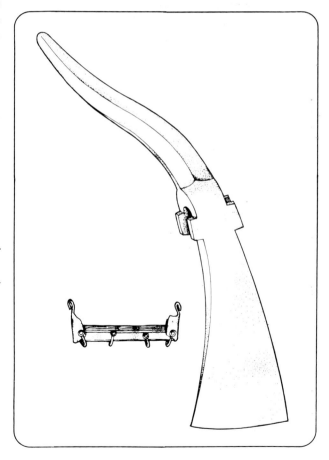

The *dolabra*—military pickaxe. These were provided with angled metal guards to cover the axe edge, tied on by means of thongs.

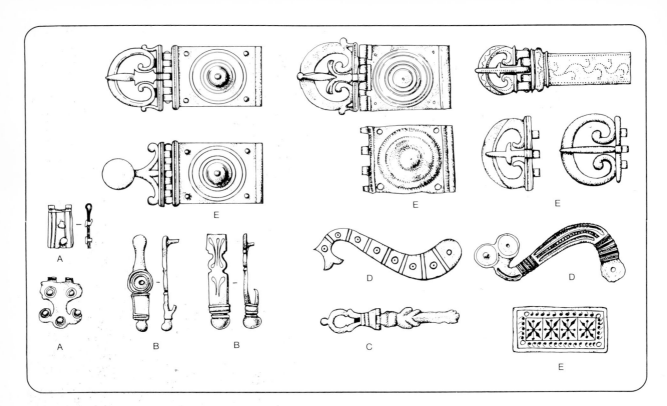

(a) **Fittings from a** *lorica segmentata*, **with crude decoration. (b) Cavalry harness decorations. (c) Baldric fastener with a hinged loop. (d) Types of breasthooks from mail shirts. (e) Belt fittings, usually tinned or silvered.**

helmets from the arms factories—a large *fabricia* could only supply six per month.

The first true cavalry helmets probably emerged during the first half of the 1st century AD and consisted of an iron skull with a deep back and iron cheek-guards, the whole being skinned over with thin embossed bronze sheet (see colour plates H1 and H2). The only specimen of one of these skinned helmets to have survived in a reasonably good state of preservation was found at Witcham Gravel in Cambridgeshire and is now in the British Museum. The steep angle and size of the neck-guard suggest that the piece was made during the third quarter of the 1st century AD.

The helmets of the auxiliary infantry, as may be seen in colour plate D2, were very much simpler than their legionary counterparts and were sometimes made by a process known today as 'metal-spinning'. The example illustrated is based on the skull found at Flüren in Germany. This method of manufacture is accomplished by forcing a disc of metal, in this case annealed bronze, over a former of either wood or metal revolving in a type of lathe. An interesting point arises in connection with this method of manufacture. We know today that a considerable amount of power is required to operate a spinning lathe and one may well wonder how the Romans managed to generate such a force. It is also known that medieval armoury workshops employed power supplied by water-wheels to turn their machinery such as large grindstones, and this practice was continued for the manufacture of agricultural implements as late as the early Industrial Revolution. Could it possibly be the case that the Romans, to whom this form of power was known, also employed it for such purposes?

The sword

The *gladius* of Caesarian to Tiberian date, with its fine broad-shouldered and long-pointed blade, while being somewhat heavy, was probably one of the most aesthetically pleasing objects the Romans ever produced, and was a descendant of the weapon of the Spanish Celts.

The hilt was made in three parts: the guard, with a recessed underside lined with a bronze plate; the grip, usually of bone; and the pommel, surmounted

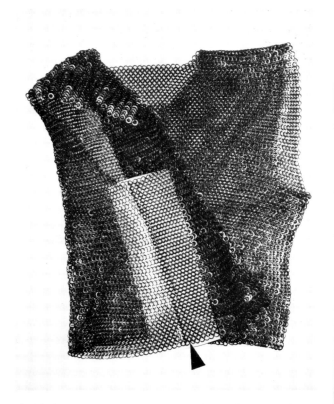

(Left) Piece of a mail hauberk of unriveted link made by the author, showing the probable position of the join discovered in the Carlingwark Loch fragment (arrowed). (Right) An entire unleathered shoulder doubling of Greek type, laid out to show expansions (arrowed) necessary to achieve a good fit. This piece of mail would have been joined to the main body of the hauberk with a single line of rings across the base of the back.

by a bronze terminal which held the parts in position on the blade's tang. The grips were usually of octagonal section, occasionally hexagonal, with four concave finger-grips carved into each of the surfaces, producing a very desirable effect which gave the soldier an excellent hold on the weapon. The guards and pommels were sometimes made from hardwood, doubtless producing a cheaper weapon than those that used ivory for these parts. A more expensive version of the hilt was found together with its blade at Rheingonheim: this was made from wood, but encased with silver plate.

The scabbard for this pattern of sword was, as is usual with scabbards, basically wooden with a leather covering sewn on while wet. This sheathing, together with a full-length face-plate, was slipped into a metal frame of side-gutters and cross-bands soldered into a terminal at the lower end; once the sheathing was in position, the scabbard was capped

with a locket which was secured with a pin driven through the back of the locket and the wooden liner, being bent over on the inside of the scabbard.

The face-plate sometimes bore decoration in the form of embossed slips which showed either side of the cross-bands and had elaborately pierced or embossed locket and chape plates. Some swords bore a roundel displaying the Emperor's image encircled with a wreath ('Sword of Tiberius', British Museum).

A slightly later pattern is represented by swords of the Fulham type (see author's reconstruction), named after the specimen recovered from the River Thames and now in the British Museum. The face-plate shown in the model does not belong to the original Fulham Sword, the scabbard of which was incomplete. These were the first swords known to have employed the parallel edges of the blade so characteristic of the later Romans. The broad shoulders remain, though the overall width has been lessened. The long point is also in evidence, but the slight and graceful curve of the Celtic ancestors has entirely disappeared. The hilt is

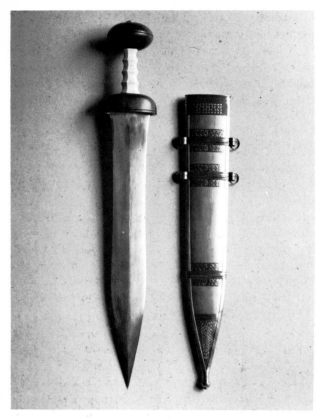

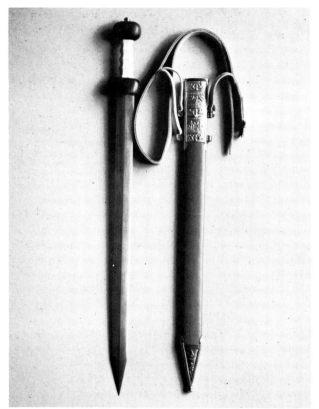

A reconstruction by the author of an infantry sword dating from the reign of Augustus Caesar, modelled on the remains of a scabbard from Mainz, with pierced decoration, and a blade of similar pattern to the badly corroded original found on the Chapel Street site, Chichester. The original blade may be seen in the Chichester District Museum.

A reconstruction by the author of a *spatha*—cavalry sword—dating from the 1st century AD, modelled on a blade found at Newstead near Melrose, Scotland, now in the National Museum of Antiquities of Scotland, and a locket of unknown provenance belonging to a weapon of this type. The belt and chape are hypothetical.

hypothetical.

During the first half of the 1st century AD and certainly before the invasion of Britain, a new pattern of *gladius* had emerged; this was to set the final shape of Roman infantry swords until barbarian influence superseded the arms and armour of Celtic origin. These swords, which we call the Pompeii pattern after the three specimens found amongst the ruins of that city (see author's reconstruction of a Pompeii-pattern sword, also the Long Windsor type), had short, strong points and completely parallel edges.

There was also a completely new form of scabbard introduced at this time, apparently for both the infantry and cavalry swords. This consisted of the normal sheath, but the side-gutters and face-plate had been made obsolete, being replaced by the separate lockets and chapes shown in the author's reconstructions. This type of

scabbard may have been the final truly Roman pattern, and despite the depiction of scabbards with side-gutters in sculpture, the older pattern was probably never reverted to.

Short swords were normally worn on the right side, and, in view of their relatively short blades, were drawn by inverting the hand to grasp the hilt and pushing the pommel forward. The scabbards obviously had to be very free to permit this method of draw; a weapon which jammed in its scabbard would have been disastrous to its owner.

The shield

The great curved legionary shield—*scutum*—is thought to have been Celtic in origin, being derived from flat oval shields made from a single layer of timber for the main shield board. The introduction of a lateral curvature would have meant the introduction of the early form of plywood described by the historian Polybius, who wrote a reasonably explicit description of the Roman army during the 2nd century BC. The early type was made from two layers of wood glued together and then covered with canvas and hide, the upper and lower edges being bound with iron. The shields of Caesar's time were probably much like that discovered at Kasr el Harit in Egypt, known as the 'Fayum Scutum'. This specimen, the only early example of a *scutum* yet discovered, was made from three layers of wooden strips and was covered with woolen felt; presumably the latter was a substitute for the canvas covering and the Fayum shield may have been formerly covered with hide, which was subsequently removed. Like most oval shields of the period, this specimen has ribs or 'spines' on the face, a feature which the Romans continued to employ up to the end of the 1st century BC.

It was probably during the second half of that century that the *scutum* underwent its first stage of alteration towards the semi-cylindrical form; the upper and lower curves were removed (see author's reconstruction), and at about the turn of the century or a little later, the shield board seems to have been made lighter; this necessitated the introduction of back-bracing, evidenced by the presence of 'L' shapes in the corners on the face of these shields (Arch of Orange and grave stele of C. Valerius Crispus).

By the middle of the 1st century AD the final semi-cylindrical *scutum* had appeared, and this seems to have remained the basic shape of the legionary shield until it was replaced in the late Empire by large circular types. An example of what is probably a late *scutum* was found at Dura-Europos on the River Euphrates. It was considered to be a piece of parade equipment for many years; however, there is nothing to support this assertion, and the Dura *scutum* represents the furthest development of the Celtic shield in the mid-3rd century, shortly before it became obsolete.

The javelin

There were, generally speaking, two types of pole weapon in the Roman army: the *hasta* or thrusting spear with a leaf-shaped blade, and the *pilum* or javelin.

Because the remains of two different patterns of javelin were found on the site of the siege of Alesia, it is considered that the legionaries of Caesar's time were still carrying two *pila* each, as they had done in the previous century—one heavy type with a large splice-block to increase its weight, and a lighter socketed type for use at longer range. However, the description of the opening of the engagement between Caesar's legions and those of Pompey the Great at Pharsalus seems to indicate the carriage of only one *pilum* per man, and it is possible that the practice had changed by that date.

By the middle of the 1st century AD the splice-type *pilum* had become lighter, judging by three specimens found in the fort at Oberaden in Germany; and a new pattern of much heavier type had also been introduced. The latter had a tapered shaft fitted with a heavy lead load just behind the slightly shorter splice-block, which held a shorter iron head than the earlier patterns. The purpose of the load was obviously to increase the penetrative ability of the weapon, and when handling this javelin it becomes clear that it was intended to be used at fairly close range. The Cancelleria Relief at Rome shows men of the Praetorian Guard parading with similar weapons which have eagle motifs cast on the loads; it is most unlikely that this would have been a feature of the common field javelin, and it is practicably possible that the Praetorians' *pila* were provided with bronze loads instead of the usual lead ones. Such an image cast on a lead object would not

The common Roman military boot used by both infantry and cavalry, shown here with a spur found at Hod Hill, Dorset. Reconstruction by the author.

have survived for very long in normal daily life; a single light blow against a wall would destroy at least part of the emblem.

It is difficult to tell whether or not each legionary carried more than one javelin at this date, for there were many different variations on the same theme; sculpture, for what it may be worth as evidence, does not show legionaries carrying more than one each, while auxiliaries are shown to carry as many as three pole weapons at once (Mainz Praetorium).

The military belt and dagger

The belt, or *cingulum militare,* as previously mentioned, began its life as a means of distributing the weight of mail onto the wearer's hips and for the carriage of the sword and dagger. During the reign of Augustus the practice was to wear two belts, one for each sidearm.

In the early 1st century AD the groin-guard, or 'sporran' as it has been called, made its appearance. Initially it was copied from the Celtic practice of cutting the tie-end of a belt into four strips, using

only one of these to fasten the belt, all four being fitted with small terminals. By the middle of the century the groin-guard had become a separate item attached to one of the belts—usually that for the dagger—and some were very elaborate affairs. The fittings of the 1st century were of enormous variety, usually being tinned or silvered; in some cases the embossed relief stamped into the thin bronze with cast dies was left unsilvered, to provide a beautiful effect against the ground. Others were inlaid with black niello, as were many cavalry harness fittings. The military belt began to go out of favour towards the end of the 1st century; there is evidence of a reduction of the groin-guard in the case of legionaries, and its total cessation of issue to the auxilia.

The dagger (*pugio*) was, like the *gladius*, of Spanish origin, and was sometimes a very well-made piece of equipment with highly ornate decoration of silver or gold with red enamel inlay on the scabbard and sometimes the hilt as well (Colchester Museum). The most common form of construction was a blade and hilt silhouette with horn applied to both sides of the hilt, probably worked to the form shown in the author's reconstruction; a skinning of either thin bronze or iron was then applied to the outside and riveted

Author's reconstruction of the Imperial Gallic type 'I' helmet from the River Rhine at Mainz. Only the skull of the original helmet survived; the cheek-guards are restored, based on a contemporary pattern. (Part of a complete equipment made by the author for the Rijksmuseum G.M. Kam, Nijmegen, Netherlands)

1: Legionary infantryman, late Republic period
2, 3: Legionary infantrymen, late Augustan to Tiberian period

A

1: Centurio, Legio II Augusta, late Augustan to Tiberian period
2: Signifer, Legio XIV Gemina, Tiberian period
3: Aquilifer, Legio XI Claudia Pia Fidelis, mid-1st C. AD

B

1: Legionary infantryman, Legio VIII Augusta, mid-1st C. AD
2: Aquilifer, Legio XIV Gemina, first half 1st C. AD
3: Centurio, Legio XI Claudia Pia Fidelis, mid-1st C. AD

C

1: Signifer, Cohors V Asturum, 1st C. AD
2: Auxiliary infantryman, mid-1st C. AD
3: Imagnifer, 1st C. AD

D

1: Centurio, Legio XX Valeria, mid-1st C. AD
2: Legionary infantryman, mid-1st C. AD
3: Legionary infantryman, second half 1st C. AD

1

2

3

E

1: Legionary infantryman, Legio II Adiutrix, late 1st C. AD
2: Auxiliary infantryman of a Cohors Equitata, Trajanic period
3: Legionary infantryman, Trajanic period

F

1: Provincial legate, early Imperial period
2: Junior tribune, early Imperial period
3: Cornicen, Trajanic period

G

1: Cavalry trooper, Ala Noricum, second half 1st C. AD
2: Cavalry trooper, Ala Noricum, mid-1st C. AD

H

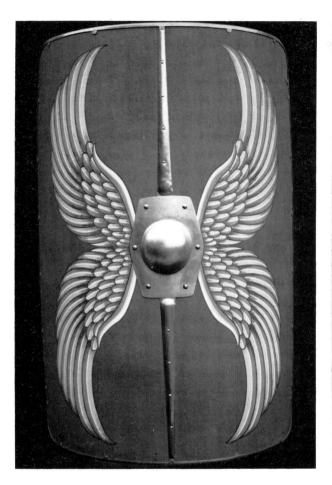

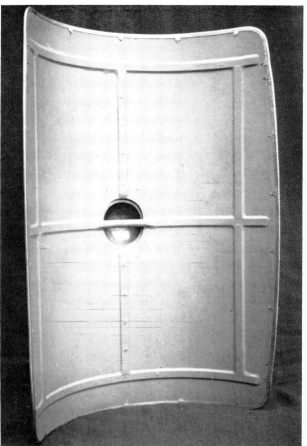

(Left) **A curve-sided** *scutum* **(hypothetical reconstruction by the author) of Augustan date. The ribs on the face are a survival from much earlier shields of this type. (Right) The back of the same shield showing bracing, thought to have been introduced during the reign of Augustus to stiffen a lighter shield-board. (Part of a complete equipment made by the author for the Riveredge Foundation, Calgary, Canada)**

through. The use of either metal would have matched that employed for the scabbard. The scabbard construction was simple, but very effective. The main plate of the scabbard was worked back round the edges and soldered to a thin back-plate. The side-rings were attached by means of nails passed right through the sides of the scabbard and simply bent over on the rear. The dagger ceased to be issued at the end of the 1st century AD.

CONCLUSION

The limitations of space in a book of this size prevent any discussion here of the course of specific campaigns fought by the Roman army in our period. These may be found in many standard works of history; and since all are based on a relatively – and tragically – fragmentary surviving body of Roman historical writing, such as Tacitus' *Annals of Imperial Rome*, which is generally available in inexpensive translations, the author must leave it to the interested reader to pursue his research elsewhere. The author's remit in this treatment is, after all, to concentrate upon the physical detail of

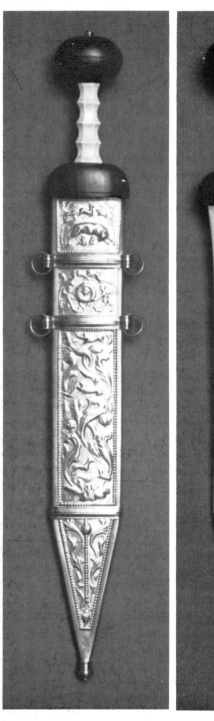

his subject, which in this case is certainly varied and fascinating enough to occupy many times the available space.

In conclusion, however, it is surely permissible to add that the debt owed today by European (and thus by extension, North American) culture and civilisation to the long-dead legionaries and auxiliaries of Rome is incalculable. Through their army the Romans not only conquered new lands, but brought the benefits of their civilisation to countries where internal warfare had been a way of life. Many of those benefits were secured through the hard work and skill of the legionaries, in their role as the only organised force of craftsmen and engineers available to the new provinces.

Though at times the Romans were responsible for some astounding cruelties, it should be remembered that most peoples of their time engaged in what we today would regard as unacceptable behaviour in civilised society. It would be an entirely distorted reading of history to believe that they were morally very different from the peoples they subjugated.

Generally speaking, the advantages to be gained from belonging to the Roman world were very great. The greatest force for happiness throughout human history, after all, has been the expectation of ordinary people that they can live their lives, tend their land and raise their children in peace. The Roman army created conditions in which, for centuries on end, a farmer could normally hope to till his fields secure in the knowledge that a marauding band from a neighbouring tribe would not be permitted to carry off the fruit of his labour, and probably to slaughter or enslave him and his family into the bargain.

Under the *Pax Romana* a man could travel from Palmyra in Syria to Eburacum in north Britain without a passport and without ever feeling entirely out of place. Wherever he went, Rome had established a miniature version of the mother city, with markets, baths, temples, and all the other complexities of the 'Roman way'. It was for the establishment of these benefits and the maintenance of that order that the Roman army was directly responsible; and though, for many different reasons, the outer fabric eventually fell into ruin, the all-important core of that experience remains with us today. So perhaps the noble Romans' wish and belief is a reality after all: ROMA AETERNA EST!

Author's reconstruction of a 'Fulham' pattern sword and scabbard. These swords are named after an incomplete specimen recovered from the River Thames. The example shown has an embossed face-plate from Germany and the original Fulham blade-form, locket, frame and terminal. This pattern was probably developed in the Roman Rhineland during the early 1st century AD, with a fairly limited production, giving way to the 'Pompeii' type during the reign of Tiberius. (In the collection of Mr. T. W. Rath, Vermont, USA)

THE PLATES

M·FAVONM·F·POL·FACI
LIS·⊃·LEG·XX·VERECVND
VS·EI·NO·VIC·SVB·POSV
ERVNT·H·S·E·

A1: Legionary infantryman, late Republic period

The reconstruction is largely based on a figure shown in the reliefs on the Altar of Domitius Ahenobarbus in the Louvre. The sculpture portrays legionaries wearing long sleeveless mail hauberks with shoulder doubling, which in this case appears to have been leathered on the face of the mail, in order that decoration could be applied.

The helmet is of Montefortino type 'C', which may be regarded as plain state issue armour, with a horse-hair crest attached to the helmet by means of a single pin inserted vertically into the knob on the crown.

The shield is the early *scutum*, measuring approximately four feet in height. Shields of this type were most probably developed from Celtic flat oak patterns which were made from a single board, tapered towards the edges. Whilst the horizontal grip and wooden boss remained the same, the Roman introduction of a lateral curve necessitated the invention of a form of plywood for the shield board.

A2: Legionary infantryman, late Augustan to Tiberian period

The body defence of this figure is based on a representation on the Arch of Orange (Arausio), which was erected in the reign of Tiberius to commemorate the suppression by Legio II Augusta of a Gallic revolt in AD 21. The main defence is again mail, but with protection to the thighs being afforded by a kilt of *pteruges*, pendant strips of hide, which have also been added to the upper arms. The *pteruges* would have been attached to an arming doublet, probably of hide, worn beneath the mail corselet. The shoulder doubling is backed and piped with hide and braced across the chest with a double

Author's reconstruction of a *lorica segmentata* **of Corbridge type 'A', found on the site of the Roman supply base of Corstopitum near to Corbridge in Northumberland. (In the collection of the Lancashire Schools Museum Service)**

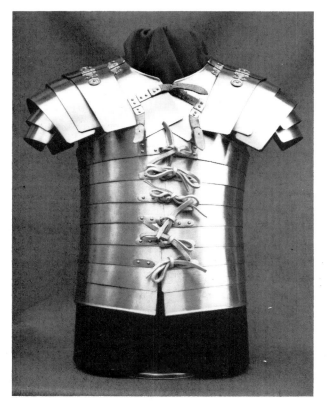

hook device; the latter prevented the doubling 'straps' from slipping outwards, their natural tendency.

The helmet is of Coolus type 'C', based on an example from Schaan, Liechtenstein. This type of head-piece was very well made, with relatively heavy frontal reinforces or 'peaks' to prevent blows from striking the helmet bowl. The fastening strap would have had slits near to the ends which were simply pressed over projecting studs on the outside of the cheek-guards. It is difficult to understand why the Romans did not make greater use of this very fast method of securing the helmet, instead of using thongs tying beneath the chin.

The shield shows the first stage of alteration towards the semi-cylindrical form of *scutum* of later periods. The top and bottom curves have been removed, reducing the height to about three feet four inches. The side curves remain, perhaps also the tapering thickness of the shield board. By this date waist belts were being worn in pairs, one for each sidearm.

A3: Legionary infantryman, late Augustan to Tiberian period

The long mail hauberk of this figure is also based on the reliefs of the Arch of Orange and appears to be the more common of the two types. The lengthening of the body of the hauberk has rendered the 'kilt' of *pteruges* unnecessary; however, they remain in the deltoid region, and it may be that the Romans had not learned to tailor their mail to make a satisfactory shoulder-cap by this date. The Gauls appear to have been able to overcome this slight problem in the manufacture of similar body defences. An excellent example is the fine statue of a late Celtic warrior from Vacheres, southern France. Presumably the upper arm *pteruges* would have still required an arming doublet.

The helmet, here shown slung for the march in friendly territory, is of Coolus type 'E' and is based on the Walbrook helmet in the British Museum. Unlike the Schaan helmets, this pattern was fitted with a solid bronze crest spike and side tubes for plumes. The central crest would have been a brush and tail of horse-hair similar to the late Republic type, but with a small crest-box to hold the hair in a more erect manner.

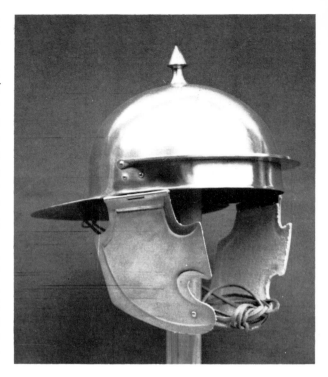

The shield is shown with its temporary goat hide cover for the march. Such covers were probably only removed for sentry duty or when an engagement was imminent. On the march, the shield was carried on a baldric, which allowed the soldier to carry his kit pole with his left hand. Experiment has shown that it is necessary to strap the shield up high in the manner shown here, in order to clear the man's legs in motion.

B1: Centurio, Legio II Augusta, late Augustan to Tiberian period

This figure also appears on the reliefs of the Arch of Orange and is easily identifiable as a centurion by his greaves. The body defence is very similar to that of figure A3, except that the centurion wears a medallion of the Gorgon Medusa suspended from the junction of the breasthooks; this was an amulet intended to protect the wearer from harm. The deep plated belt worn at the midriff may also be peculiar to the rank of centurion, since it is to be encountered again on the stele of the centurion Marcus Favonius Facilis (see plate E1) at Colchester.

The helmet shown on the sculpture has no transverse crest, as might have been expected, and the helmet itself is rather too stylised for the precise

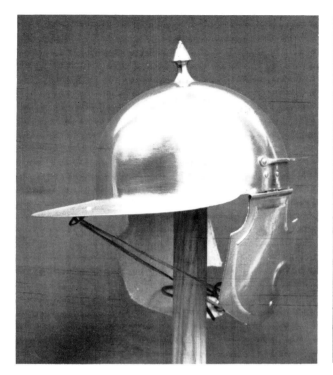

Reconstruction by the author of a Coolus type 'E' helmet of the late Augustan period. Helmets of this type appear to have been relegated to the auxiliaries as more advanced forms of armour were issued to the legions. (Riveredge Foundation, Calgary, Canada)

pattern to be identified. The helmet shown in this reconstruction is based on the remains of a bronze skull of Coolus type 'F' found in Bosham harbour and a cheek-guard found at Hod Hill in Dorset.

The *scutum* shown with the figure on the Arch of Orange displays in one corner a small 'L' shape, perhaps the earliest representation of what is thought to be a reinforcing washer for the corner of back-braces, which in turn may indicate the development of a lighter shield construction. The shield boss is of interlamination type, i.e. it was provided with a narrow flange which was set in between the laminations of the shield board during manufacture.

B2: Signifer, Legio XIV Gemina, Tiberian period

The grave stele upon which this figure is based shows a mail hauberk with a shoulder doubling more usually associated with Roman cavalry in the 1st century AD; however, mail capes had been known among the Celts in earlier periods, and the influence of Celtic armaments upon those of the Romans is undeniable. This influence may also extend into religious practice as far as standard bearers are concerned, in connection with their now-obvious employment of what have become known as 'sports' helmets because of their association with the *Hippika Gymnasia*. The soldier also wears heavier defences of *pteruges*, both in the kilt and upper arms; again, one would expect these to have been carried by an arming doublet beneath the corselet.

The military belt carrying the dagger is also fitted with a large groin-guard or 'sporran', as it is sometimes called today. These extra defences were introduced in the early 1st century AD and were probably developed from Gallic belts with multiple terminations (see plate C2).

Resting upon the left shoulder of the figure on the grave stele is what can only be a masked helmet with a pointed diadem, bearing a very distinct resemblance to the bronze cavalry 'sports' helmet skull found at Newstead in Scotland; as already mentioned, it is most probably of significance in relation to the standard bearer's position as guardian of an object of spiritual importance. Whether or not this helmet would have been exchanged for a normal field head-piece for battle is impossible to say with any certainty; however, such

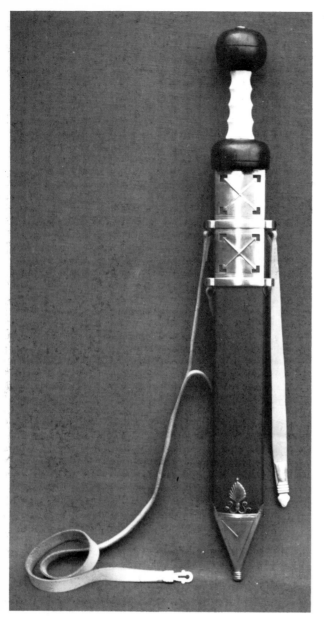

Author's reconstruction of what was probably a common issue type of 'Pompeii' pattern infantry sword, employing the scabbard mounts said to have been found at Long Windsor, Dorset, now in the Ashmolean Museum, Oxford. (Part of a complete equipment for the Hertfordshire Schools)

'sports' helmets would not have provided the best defence available.

B3: Aquilifer, Legio XI Claudia Pia Fidelis, mid-1st century AD

This figure is based on the grave stele of Lucius Sertorius Firmus in the Verona Museum, whose legion received its formal title in AD 42 for remaining loyal to the Emperor Claudius during a revolt in Dalmatia.

The body defence of scales is called a *lorica plumata* in this instance, because the spined scales resemble feathers. The upper arm defences and kilt of *pteruges* carry fringing, a feature which appears to have been reserved for *principales* (the Senior 'NCO' grades) and above during the 1st and probably the 2nd centuries AD. An arming doublet would be used to support the *pteruges*.

The helmet and pelt drape are presumed. In Roman sculpture, eagle bearers are usually shown bare-headed; indeed, there is to date no known example of a helmeted *aquilifer*. However, even if the eagle bearer, for some religious or other reason, normally went without headgear of any kind, it might be expected that a helmet was worn in action, especially by a man who was frequently exposed to extremes of peril in battle.

The figure on the stele carries a shield on his back by means of a baldric, and though the shield is not visible it would most probably be a *parma*, a relatively small circular pattern which could be carried easily without use of the hands.

C1: Legionary infantryman, Legio VIII Augusta, mid-1st century AD.

The figure is based on the grave stele of Caius Valerius Crispus in the Stadtisches Museum, Wiesbaden (see photo of stele). The main body defences are almost identical to those of B2, except that the shoulder doubling is of the Greek cut as opposed to the 'cape'. The mail is tightly belted at the waist with a deep military belt fitted with a long groin-guard.

The sword is suspended by means of a baldric, which appeared during the first half of the 1st century AD as a replacement for one of the two elaborate belts, though the practice of wearing a sword belt did not cease completely.

The shield back shows the bracing thought to have been introduced late in the reign of Augustus. As may be seen on the original stele; the shield face bears 'L'-shaped pieces in the corners, which are probably intended to be metals, since all the painted parts of the device which would very likely have been present on the original carving have disappeared over the centuries.

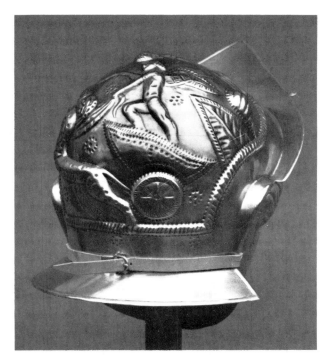

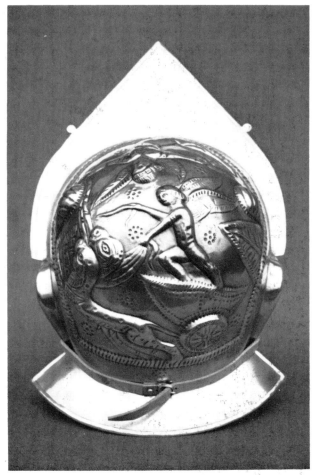

Two views of the author's reconstruction of a bronze cavalry 'sports' helmet skull of type 'B' found at Newstead near Melrose, Scotland. Helmets of this type are shown on the grave stelae of standard bearers (see colour plates). (Author's collection)

The helmet is of the type denoted Imperial Italic 'C', which is dated to the end of the second quarter and the third quarter of the 1st century AD. At this time crests would have been worn for ceremonials such as the legion's birthday celebrations, when the Eagle standard was dressed with garlands.

C2: Aquilifer, Legio XIV Gemina, first half of the 1st century AD

The figure is based on the grave stele of Gnaius Musius in the Mittelrheinisches Landesmuseum, Mainz. He is wearing what is probably a ceremonial attire, since no practical form of corselet is visible. He wears a jerkin, perhaps of hide with *pteruges* attached, over which is strapped a harness bearing his *donae*, won during his service—though the Romans did make posthumous awards.

The decorations consist of two *torques* or Celtic collars and nine *phalerae*. A further award, probably originating from Celtic spoils, is the *armilla* or bracelet worn on the right wrist. The wearing of bracelets by men was confined to the military; in civil life, the Romans considered them as purely female adornment.

The soldier also wears a military belt with the earliest form of groin-guard, the strap-end simply cut into four strips with small terminals attached, and only one strip being used to fasten the belt.

In action, Musius would probably have worn a corselet of fine mail or scale and some protection to the head, as already discussed in relation to plate B3.

C3: Centurio, Legio XI Claudia Pia Fidelis, mid-1st century AD

The figure is based on the grave stele of Quintus Sertorius Festus in the Verona Museum—possibly a contemporary relative of Lucius Sertorius Firmus. The centurion is shown in what would be ceremonial dress. He wears a scale defence with two layers of scallops to the lower edge, and single layers of *pteruges* in both the kilt and upper arm defences. Over these are his decorations consisting of nine large, elaborately embossed *phalerae* mounted on a

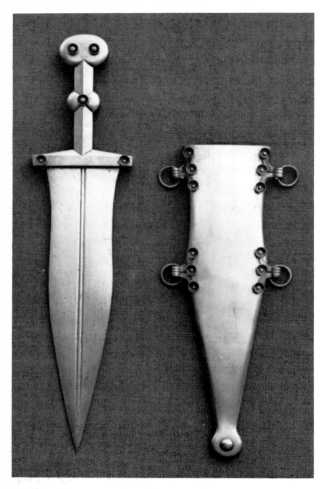

Infantry dagger and scabbard—author's reconstruction. These sidearms were usually engraved and inlaid with silver or gold and red enamel. The dagger ceases to be in evidence after the end of the 1st century AD, but re-emerges in the 3rd century as a much larger but rather poorer quality piece.

harness, two *torques*, and on his head a wreath perhaps of gilded oak leaves, a *corona civica* (the original stone is too badly damaged in this area for the wreath to be positively identified, and it may be the *corona aurea*).

The man wears a pair of embossed greaves, which were peculiar to the rank of centurion by this date. The vine staff was also symbolic of the centurionate, but had a more practical application—on the backs of the centurion's charges.

In Caesar's time it was practice to wear decorations for combat; however, it seems rather unlikely that the very beautiful *phalerae* (such as the exquisite set found near Xanten in lower Germany and known as the Lauersfort Phalerae) would have been subjected to such treatment, unless the object of visual splendour was considered to be necessary at a particular moment.

D1: Signifer, Cohors V Asturum, 1st century AD

The figure is based on the grave stele of Pintaius in the Rheinisches Landesmuseum, Bonn. The body defence is a short mail hauberk with a band of hide at the lower edge supporting a fringe, and belted at the waist with a pair of military belts, one for each sidearm. The stele shows the belts to be arranged in a horizontal fashion, which is unusual, and may be the individual sculptor's or workshop's practice.

The pelt draping the helmet has clearly had its mask removed, a feature which can also be associated with plate D3. A possible explanation for this may be found in the non-citizen status of the unit or of the soldier concerned.

The studs on the groin-guard are not visible on the stele, and it has been assumed that here, as in other cases, these small details would have been represented in paint which has now disappeared.

D2: Auxiliary infantryman, mid-1st century AD

The figure is partly based on the stele of Annaius Daverzus, who served with the 4th Dalmatian Infantry Cohort. The figure wears the simplest type of Roman mail hauberk, with short sleeves and probably a draw-lace at the neck opening; it had a weight of approximately 14lbs.

The belts and elaborate groin-guard are based on those of Daverzus' grave stele and are, judging by archaeological finds, a suprisingly accurate sculptural representation. Daverzus himself may well have been of citizen status, since he is shown on the stele to have what is thought to be a bronze diploma, tucked into his tunic just above the belts.

The helmet is a cheap spun type, the skull having been found at Flüren and matched with a cheek-guard from Büderich. The simplicity of this piece must clearly indicate that it belonged to an auxiliary soldier, although the skull bears no inscription to attest the fact.

The soldier carries the normal auxiliary's shield, the oval *clipeus*, and a thrusting spear. A rather crude relief from the Vespasianic Praetorium at Mainz shows one of these men also carrying two light javelins as well as the spear.

D3: Imagnifer, 1st century AD

The figure is based on a cast of the grave stele of Genialis, *imagnifer* of the 7th Raetian Infantry Cohort, in the Römisch-Germanisches Zentralmuseum, Mainz. The body defence of mail is fitted with a cape doubling over the shoulders, fastened with the normal breasthooks, and a pair of belts for the sidearms.

The stele shows the man bare-headed with his pelt and helmet resting on his left shoulder. Protruding from the pelt is the pointed diadem of a sports helmet skull with its mask removed. Comparing this feature with the *signifer* of Legio XIV Gemina (plate B2), it appears that standard bearers of non-citizen status also wore 'sports' helms for specific purposes, but had the mask removed, perhaps because of their status; the same seems to be the case with the animal pelt shown on plate D1. The imago itself was a portrait of the Emperor or a member of his family. In action, assuming the *imagnifer* became involved in the fray, he may have worn a more serviceable helmet.

E1: Centurio, Legio XX Valeria, mid-1st century AD

The figure is based on the grave stele of Marcus Favonius Facilis in the Colchester and Essex Museum, Colchester. The body defence has extensions in the deltoid region which have helped to definitely identify such corselets as mail and not leather, as many have in the past supposed. For the successful manufacture of these extensions, it is necessary to employ mailmaker's constructions which have not previously been attributed to the Romans; though why it should have been considered that the Romans were incapable of understanding one or two elementary methods of tailoring mail, which they would doubtless have learned from the Celts, is difficult to comprehend. On the stele the corselet is shown to have been edged at all three extremities, and has shoulder doubling straps which are rather longer than usual.

Experiments with the author's full-scale reconstruction, now in the Museum at Colchester, have proved that the *pteruges* must have been mounted on an arming doublet beneath the mail and were not actually attached to the corselet itself.

The greaves represented on the stele are plain, but since parts of the sculpture are known to have been finished out with gesso and would doubtless

have been painted, these pieces may well have been decorated with an embossed design.

While the stele does not depict a helmet, iron head-pieces were becoming fairly widespread at the time of Facilis' death (thought to be between AD 43 and 49) and he may possibly have owned one, but he could equally well have been helmeted in bronze; at this date, a transverse crest is to be expected. To date there is no known specimen of a helmet with attachments for such a crest, but they were probably no different from those of the ordinary infantry helmets, with only the position altered.

The lack of decorations (*dona*) on this stele does show that unlike some modern armies, the Romans did not give away awards with the rations, and here is one ordinary centurion who never managed to distinguish himself. Perhaps he was a junior officer who had entered the centurionate by direct commission and died fairly young.

Auxiliary's belt and groin-guard. The buckle and belt-plates are based on pieces found at Hod Hill, Dorset, now in the Durden Collection. (Part of a complete equipment made by the author for the Corinium Museum, Cirencester)

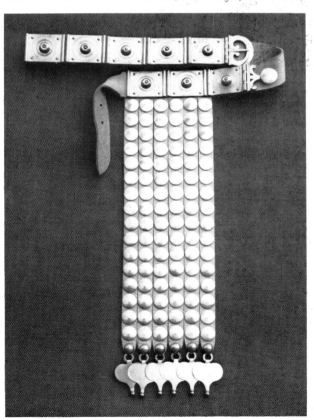

E2: Legionary infantryman, mid-1st century AD

The figure's equipment is a compilation of contemporary pieces from various sites, and is intended to represent a legionary as he might have looked late in the reign of Tiberius, when most of his equipment was developed.

The cuirass is of Corbridge type 'A', with strap fasteners between the shoulder sections and the girdles, and eight pairs of girdle plates. The helmet is of Imperial Gallic type 'E', based on a fairly well preserved skull-piece from the fort at Valkenburg, Holland. The fittings of the sword scabbard are reconstructed from the remains said to have been found at Long Windsor, Dorset; they were probably found originally on the site of the fort at Waddon Hill in the same county, and are now in the Ashmolean Museum. The javelin is of the type from the fort at Oberaden in Germany, where three good specimens of this 1st-century weapon were found. The method of covering and carrying the shield

Reconstruction of the *vexillum* **said to have been found in a grave in Egypt, the original flag now in the Museum of Fine Arts, Moscow. The side pendant terminals are based on an example found in the streambed of the Walbrook, London.**

seems to have remained the same, and it might be expected that many a damaged shoulder-splint hinge was caused by this practice.

E3: Legionary infantryman, second half of the 1st century AD

The equipment shown on this figure is again compiled from various sources, and represents a legionary from the late second quarter onward.

The cuirass is of Corbridge type 'B', which had hook and loop connectors between the shoulder sections and girdles, and only seven pairs of girdle plates instead of eight. It is possible that this type of cuirass was in manufacture and being issued by the early AD 40s, since a plate from a hinged shoulder-splint conforming very much more closely to the pattern of 'B' type was quite recently excavated from the site of the invasion supply base of Legio II Augusta at Chichester, which was occupied during the first five years of the invasion of Britain. The plate in question shows no signs of ever having been fitted to a cuirass.

The javelin is a new type with a large lead weight to increase the weapon's degree of penetration, a feature which continues into the late Empire, until the heavy javelin disappeared altogether. The helmet is of Imperial Gallic type 'F', based on the virtually complete example from the amphitheatre at Besançon, now in the Besançon Museum. The mounts on the sword scabbard are from Germany, but are of a very similar type to those found with the remains of three swords on the site of Pompeii, from which site these swords have gained their modern name.

F1: Legionary infantryman, Legio II Adiutrix, late 1st century AD

The figure is based on the grave stele of Caius Castricius in the Aquincum Museum, Budapest. The body defences appear to be very like those of the earlier years of the 1st century AD, and may provide us with a vivid example of the Roman policy of issuing equipment in a serviceable condition regardless of its age. However, the practice of doubling up the thickness of mail on the shoulders, for both infantry and cavalry, has ceased; it was probably regarded as unnecessary extra weight, of which any reduction would have been welcomed by the infantry, no doubt.

The stele shows the soldier wearing his helmet with cresting of both a horse-hair brush and side-plumes, though the forepart of the helmet has been retracted to expose the entire face and some of the man's hair. The helmet used in the reconstruction is of Imperial Gallic type 'I', recovered from the River Rhine at Mainz (see author's reconstruction). The original helmet belonged to a legionary serving with Legio I Adiutrix, a legion raised at the same date as that of Castricius.

Another unusual piece of equipment displayed on the stele is an oval shield with a boss clearly worked to represent a face, probably the Gorgon Medusa. A remarkably similar boss was found in Holland and is now in the Rijksmuseum G.M. Kam, Nijmegen; it has been copied for this colour plate.

Whether or not sword baldrics were frequently studded in the manner shown is impossible to tell; however, the stele of Castricius shows this in clear detail, but as usual omits the baldric fastener. Others may, of course, have been represented in paint and since lost.

Author's reconstruction of an auxiliary type 'A' spun helmet based on the original bronze skull in the Rheinisches Landesmuseum, Bonn, with cheek-guards of Büderich type. (Corinium Museum, Cirencester)

F2: Auxiliary infantryman of a Cohors Equitata, Trajanic period

This soldier was almost the lowest rank in the Roman army. His body defence is a simple mail hauberk which could be either plain, or 'dagged' as shown at its extremities. His legs are protected from the cold by what were probably called *bracae*, the long trousers which the Romans normally associated with the barbarian nations, giving rise to the derogatory term *bracati*. He is wearing *perones* on his feet, which are a more suitable form of footwear for cold climates, and it may be considered that these were much more widely used than appears to be the case by a mere survey of sculptural representations.

The helmet, of Auxiliary Infantry type 'C', was simple but very sturdy, and of warlike appearance in its coldly efficient design. The reconstruction is based on the skull-piece in the Museo Archaeologico, Florence, which has had its neck-guard and part of the nape cut away at a later date and a series of holes punched all the way round the base of the skull for the attachment of a lining; the latter is clearly not Roman work, since they always glued their linings in position. Many helmets of this kind may be seen in stylised form on Trajan's Column.

His sword would obviously be of the cheapest variety available, probably with an all-wooden hilt and very basic scabbard mounts and baldric fastener, such as the specimen found at Newstead in Scotland.

F3: Legionary infantryman, Trajanic period

The equipment shown on this figure is mainly based on finds from two sites: the cuirass plates from Newstead in Scotland, and the helmet from Brigetio on the Danube, near Budapest. The cuirass is considerably altered by this date. Gone are all the hinges and buckle fasteners, and the primary shoulder-guard splint is now a single plate instead of three. The collar is made from a total of six plates and has a larger, more comfortable neck-opening. The collar halves are fastened together by loops and pins which prevent any movement of the collar opening. There appears to have been a fourth type of cuirass, with laminations extending all the way up to the neck, front and rear; however, the evidence is as yet purely sculptural and finds are awaited to prove the method of construction.

The groin-guard is only half the length of the earlier type (Trajan's Column) and the dagger seems to have been made obsolete.

The helmet from the Brigetio fort, denoted Imperial Gallic type 'J', the remains of which are in the possession of the Tower of London, has a good deep neck-guard and a well-formed skull, with a peak which is angled slightly upward. The cheek-guards were of an angular pattern almost identical to a specimen found at Chester, England. So alike are they that the equipment must have originated from the same workshop.

G1: Provincial legate, early Imperial period

The figure is based on relatively common sculptures of the period, of which there must originally have been a vast number produced for circulation throughout the Empire, many of which would have been destroyed when a particular individual fell from grace. These works usually show *pteruges* employed in double layers at the deltoids and sometimes a triple layer for the 'kilt', one layer being very much shorter than the other two. These were presumably attached to an arming doublet. Over this would be worn either a short muscle cuirass (of the type portrayed) if the man was to be mounted on a horse, or one of infantry type which had an abdominal extension, usually with a row of decorated lappets protruding below the corselet. The embossed figures and designs on the armour were either raised out of the plate, or sometimes applied pieces attached with small rivets. The helmet is an example, from Autun in France, of what must surely be a senior officer's parade helmet; it was certainly not intended for use in combat. The neck-guard is laminated and has three internal leathers.

G2: Junior tribune, early Imperial period

This officer's rank is determined by the narrow stripe on his tunic, which meant that he was of Equestrian status (*tribunus augusticlavius*). There were five of these officers serving with a legion, and one senior tribune (*tribunus laticlavius*) who wore a broad stripe to signify that he was about to enter the Senate.

The figure wears knee breeches which were probably called *feminalia*, a word derived from *femen*—the lesser-known Latin word for the thigh. These garments are seen to be common to *principales* and all higher ranks, and to all the auxiliaries, both horse and foot, on Trajan's Column, but are not worn by the legionary infantry; precisely why remains an open question. No doubt the muscle cuirass worn by this officer would have been less ornate than that of the legate, especially in parade equipment, though the tribunes also wore a knotted sash around the corselet as a symbol of rank.

The helmet is hypothetical, based on an embossed representation. The brow-plate, however, is copied from an example in the Rijksmuseum, Leiden. Such helmets of Attic form are frequently portrayed in Roman sculpture and clearly did exist; however, a reasonably complete specimen has yet to be discovered.

G3: Cornicen, Trajanic period

The figure is based on representations of horn-players on Trajan's Column. The soldier wears a *lorica squamata* of quite fine scale, worked into lappets at its extremities and edged with hide. The scales were probably stitched to a foundation of coarse linen, similar to a recently discovered portion of a Severan scale corselet from Carpow, Scotland, which is backed with two-over-one linen twill. The helmet is of Imperial Italic type 'G', after the specimen said to have been found in a cave at Hebron, Israel. The original helmet is now in the Israel Museum, Jerusalem. The *cornu* itself was a very old instrument, perhaps of Etruscan origin. The Roman version probably had a high-pitched sound, in order that it could be heard above the din of battle. The *cornu* was also used in civil life; a mosaic at Nennig, District of Saarburg, shows a *cornu* being played in conjunction with an organ as accompaniment to gladiatorial combat.

H1: Cavalry trooper, Ala Noricum, second half of the 1st century AD

The figure is based on the grave stele of Titus

Reconstruction by the author of a 'Pompeii' pattern infantry sword and scabbard. Weapons of this type appeared during the first half of the 1st century AD, certainly prior to the invasion of Britain. Elaborate decoration of this kind was apparently common, though there was a simpler type represented by the Long Windsor fragments. (Part of a complete equipment now in the Rijksmuseum G.M. Kam, Nijmegen, Netherlands)

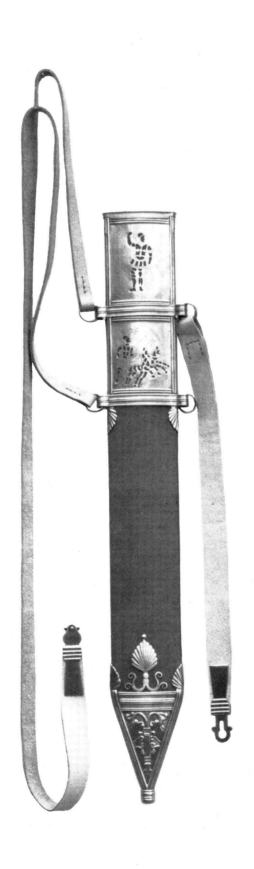

Flavius Bassus, who served in the *turma* of Fabius Pudens in the Flavian period. The stele was found at Cologne and is now in the Römisch-Germanisches Museum, Cologne. The trooper is shown wearing the common mail hauberk without sleeves and with a doubling cape. The mail has short slits at the sides to allow greater comfort in the saddle. The helmet is based on a fragmentary specimen found at Koblenz-Bubenheim, and probably represents the second stage of the development of Roman cavalry head-pieces. The large, flat, projecting peak is peculiar to the cavalry, as are cheek-guards with embossed ears which fit into the ear recesses in the helmet's skull-piece. All the helmets of this class are iron helmets primarily, decorated with thin embossed bronze skinning; part of the skinning was silvered as shown. The soldier wears *feminalia*, which appear to have been common to all cavalrymen of the 1st century and later. He also wears the same pattern of boots as the infantry, with the addition of simple prick-spurs.

The main weapon of the cavalryman was the thrusting-spear, which could be used couched as a lance, wielded over-arm to stab, or quite possibly thrown at adversaries, the rider then returning to his own lines to be replenished by his attendant (who is often portrayed in the rear of the trooper on grave stelae, carrying two or more spears). The cavalry sword of this date was not a particularly weighty weapon, rather to be regarded as a back-up to the spears. Apart from its greater length of blade this *spatha* is essentially similar to the infantry sword.

The harness of the cavalry ponies was obviously quite heavily decorated with ornaments, since a very large quantity of these fittings have been found on many of the sites where cavalry units had been present. It may be expected that the cavalry *alae* were more smartly fitted out than the equestrian section of a *cohors equitata*.

H2: Cavalry trooper, Ala Noricum, mid-1st century AD
The figure is based on the grave stele of Caius Romanius, who served in the *turma* of Claudius Capito. The stele may be seen in the Mittelrheinisches Landesmuseum, Mainz. While the stele provides no clue as to whether the body defence of this man was mail or scale armour, the use of scale by the cavalry appears to have been fairly common, and this type of armour could just as easily have been painted onto the sculpture as would have been the case with a representation of mail.

The helmet is based on fragments from various locations, largely the lower Rhine area. It is clear from the finds that a large proportion of cavalry head-pieces of this date were not fitted with a peak such as that shown on the Koblenz specimen. The Witcham Gravel helmet in the collection of the

A gate and section of turf and timber rampart reconstructed in its original position at the Lunt Fort, Baginton, near Coventry. The original fort was built shortly after the Boudican Revolt of AD 60-61, and may have been a training base for cavalry mounts.

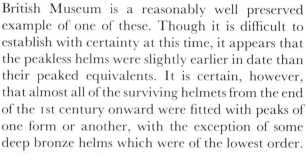

British Museum is a reasonably well preserved example of one of these. Though it is difficult to establish with certainty at this time, it appears that the peakless helms were slightly earlier in date than their peaked equivalents. It is certain, however, that almost all of the surviving helmets from the end of the 1st century onward were fitted with peaks of one form or another, with the exception of some deep bronze helms which were of the lowest order.

The pony's harness bears small cast bronze decorations along the breech and breastbands; these objects, a considerable number of which survive, have often been incorrectly identified as fittings from infantry groin-guards—or, to use archaeological parlance, 'apron terminals'. Judging by the height of several surviving bronze saddlehorn stiffener plates and the remains of saddle leathers, it appears that Roman saddles were fitted with a fairly thick cushion and would certainly have required a pair of girths.

Two views of the author's hypothetical reconstruction of a mid-1st century cavalry trooper's helmet, based on fragments from Nijmegen and Leiden. The helmet has an iron skull and cheek-guards, skinned with embossed bronze. (Author's collection)

Bibliography

H. R. Robinson: *The Armour of Imperial Rome* (1975)
G. Webster: *The Roman Imperial Army* (1969)
Peter Connolly: *Greece and Rome at War* (1981)
Peter Connolly: *The Roman Army* (1975)
Robert F. Evans: *Legions of Imperial Rome—An Informal Order of Battle Study* (1980)
V. A. Maxfield: *The Military Decorations of the Roman Army* (1981)
Polybius: *The Histories*—Loeb (1967)

BESTSELLING MILITARY AND AVIATION SERIES FROM OSPREY

MEN-AT-ARMS

An unrivalled source of information on the uniforms and insignia of fighting units throughout history. Each 48-page book includes over 40 photographs and diagrams, and eight pages of full-color artwork.

NEW VANGUARD

Comprehensive histories of the design, development and operational use of the world's armoured vehicles and artillery. Each 48-page book contains eight pages of full-color artwork including a detailed cutaway.

WARRIOR

Definitive analysis of the appearance, weapons, equipment, tactics, character and conditions of service of the individual fighting man throughout history. Each 64-page book includes full-color uniform studies in close detail, and sectional artwork of the soldier's equipment.

ELITE

Detailed information on the organization, appearance and fighting record of the world's most famous military bodies. This series of 64-page books each contains some 50 photographs and diagrams and 10 full-color plates.

CAMPAIGN

Concise, authoritative accounts of history's decisive military encounters. Each 96-page book contains over 90 illustrations including maps, orders of battle, color plates, and three-dimensional battle maps.

ORDER OF BATTLE

The most detailed information ever published on the units which fought history's great battles. Each 96-page book contains comprehensive organization diagrams supported by ultra-detailed color maps. Each title also includes a large fold-out base map.

AIRCRAFT OF THE ACES

Focuses exclusively on the elite pilots of major air campaigns, and includes unique interviews with surviving aces. Each 96-page volume contains up to 40 specially commissioned color artworks, unit listings, new scale plans and the best archival photography available.

COMBAT AIRCRAFT

Technical information from the world's leading aviation writers on the century's most significant military aircraft. Each 96-page volume contains up to 40 specially commissioned color artworks, unit listings, new scale plans and the best archival photography available.